The Billboard Guide to Writing and Producing Songs That Sell

The Billboard Guide to Writing and Producing Songs That Sell

How to Create Hits in Today's Music Industry

Eric Beall

BILLBOARD BOOKS

An Imprint of Watson-Guptill Publications

New York

Published in the United States by Watson-Guptill Publications, an imprint of the Crown Publishing Group, a division of Random House, Inc., New York.

www.crownpublishing.com

www.watsonguptill.com

Library of Congress Control Number: 2008932376

ISBN-10: 0-8230-9954-7

ISBN-13: 978-0-8230-9954-2

1 2 3 4 5 6 7 8 9 / 15 14 13 12 11 10 9

First Edition

Printed in the United States

Contents

PART THREE

WRITE YOUR OWN HIT

Acknowledgments

With heartfelt thanks to all of the songwriters, producers, artists, and music executives who share their time, talent, and expertise every day, in this crazy game of making hits.

With much appreciation to Tyler Robins and Lisa-Marie Smith for their invaluable assistance.

And with special gratitude to my wife, Cheryl, and my parents, who've been there each step of the way.

Introduction

No one really knows how many songwriters there are in the United States. We do know that there are roughly 300,000 writer-members of the three primary performing rights organizations—BMI, ASCAP, and SESAC. These are the groups that collect royalty income for songwriters whose work is played on the radio or television. The figure expands significantly when you add the countless aspiring writers who've not yet had their work played anywhere, kids in garage bands across the nation, or your uncle Harry, who's busy concocting another party-stopping ditty for next year's holiday get-together.

Suffice it to say, whether you're an accomplished professional, an amateur with grand ambitions, or a musical weekend warrior, you are not alone. There's close to half a million people out there who share the dream.

At the same time, a glance at *Billboard* magazine on any given week reveals roughly 275 singles on the major charts (country, urban, pop, rock, and Latin). Each week, approximately twenty of those songs are new releases, hitting one of the charts for the first time. Some will have staying power and continue to climb upward as their popularity increases. Others will drop off the charts a week later, never to be heard from again. Nevertheless, that's about a thousand new songs entering the charts each year.

Given those numbers, you would hardly expect to find people in the music industry wanting for songs. If there's only room for a thousand titles on the charts annually, the industry hardly needs 500,000 songwriters to supply them. In the very best of cases, less than 1 percent of the songwriters in the country will have charting singles in any given year.

Yet if one were to pick up the phone this afternoon and call a handful of music industry professionals—record company presidents, producers, publishers, or artist managers—and ask them what they need, the same reply would come back, over and over again: "Songs! I need a song for…"

This is not conjecture. As an A&R person, the notorious music-business executive responsible for selecting the material an artist should record, I know firsthand the constant pressure to unearth new songs. Indeed, even after twelve to eighteen months of working on an album, after the recording of twenty, thirty, even as many as ninety songs during the process, many labels and artists are forced to postpone record releases and put projects on hold, while the search continues for "just one more song…"

What's going on here? Why would an industry find itself searching desperately for the one thing it would seem to have plenty of, all

while songwriters face overwhelming odds in the quest to ha.
of their songs recorded? The answer lies in a breakdown in the chain
of supply and demand. The songwriters are supplying the songs.
The industry is demanding something else entirely.

No artist, manager, or A&R person searches for just any song.
None searches for even a good song. Everyone is looking for a *hit*
song. Unfortunately, most songwriters, and many A&R people,
don't exactly know what a hit song is. Fewer still have figured out
how to construct one.

This is the bad news. The good news is that for those select few
who have studied the craft of songwriting long enough to discern
what separates great from good, the rewards are high indeed.

Let's take another look at *Billboard*. In examining the writer
credits on those 275 charting singles in any particular week, we will
find the same names cropping up more than once. In fact, there are
usually twenty-five to thirty writers who have more than one song
on the charts at the same time. This is quite remarkable.

If the chances of landing even one song on the charts are less
than 1 percent, how can twenty-five to thirty people each week
have several? In fact, some top writers may have three or four songs
charting simultaneously.

What explains this? Is it simply a matter of exceptional talent?
Certainly, that must be one factor. But most of us in the record
business have seen dozens of immensely gifted people release
highly touted records and fail to achieve even a glimmer of
commercial success. Talent alone is not a ticket to the top of the
Hot 100. Is it luck? Doubtful. Luck may land a songwriter one
successful song, once in his or her career, but it won't put four
songs on the chart in the same week.

If you've ever tried to meet someone at a restaurant whom you're seeing for the first time, you've learned that it helps to have an idea of what he or she looks like. Knowledge is power, and that's especially true when you're chasing something as elusive as a hit song. Songwriters who turn up on the charts again and again know something that most others do not. They understand what makes a hit record. Once they have that knowledge, they can repeat the success that escapes 99 percent of their peers.

The primary objective of *The Billboard Guide to Writing and Producing Songs That Sell* is to give you the information you need to go from being a "songwriter" to a "hit maker." Whether you are a novice or have been working at your craft for years, to create songs that sell, you have to understand and recognize the nature of a hit song, the role it plays in the music industry, and what it takes to put a song on the radio or to turn an unknown artist into a superstar. No matter what genre you call your own, be it pop, rock, country, hip-hop, R&B, or adult contemporary, you must adapt the perspective of a chart-topping writer and producer and discover the time-tested formulas that lie at the heart of commercial success.

This is not a book about the fundamental technique of songwriting. There are more than enough of those already in existence, and I would encourage you to study them. Our goal is to reinterpret the basics of composition and lyric writing, by approaching each step with the insight and exacting standards of an industry professional. Then we'll go even further, to examine the all-important hook, where melody, lyric, and rhythm combine to create the twist that can turn your song into a hit.

But can it be done? Aren't we really trying to capture lightning in a bottle? Isn't the process by which something gains the fickle favor of the public really a mystery, even to those responsible for putting the wheels in motion? Some would certainly have us believe so.

Brandon Tartikoff, the legendary television executive responsible for *The Cosby Show, Miami Vice, Cheers,* and *LA Law,* once said, "All hits are flukes." This is not an uncommon sentiment in the record business as well. Ask A&R people to define a hit, and many will raise their eyebrows and assure you that there's no formula and that no one can really predict what will be successful. The irony is that the person telling you this is paid a substantial salary precisely because of his or her supposed ability to pick hits. If hits are entirely random and unpredictable, a company hardly needs a staff of executives to go out and find them.

The truth is, those who have long-term success in the music industry do so by picking hit songs and artists with at least some frequency. There must be more than guesswork involved. Through the years, most thriving record executives, managers, and publishers inevitably develop some method by which they can measure a song's chances for success. And while no two people's criteria will be exactly the same, the final judgments reached by industry insiders are often remarkably uniform as to a song's strengths, weaknesses, and overall potential in the marketplace.

The problem is that many people in the industry can't articulate the factors that determine their judgments. That old fallback, "I'll know it when I hear it," simply means that for many decision makers in the music business, the process of picking hits is more unconscious than conscious.

For the songwriter faced with the challenge of creating those winning songs, luck and instinct are not enough. By uncovering the logic behind the intuition, and defining the elements that determine commercial success, *The Billboard Guide to Writing and Producing Songs That Sell* can not only help you to understand exactly what a hit song is, but it can show you how to write one, with the craftsmanship and confidence of a proven hit maker.

In Part One, "How a Song Becomes a Hit," we'll explore areas usually ignored in books about songwriting: the worlds of A&R, radio, and music marketing. In these arenas, the decisions are made as to which songs get heard and which artists break through to success. Before you start writing or rewriting, it's essential to learn what a record label A&R person, a radio music director, or music marketer needs for your song to succeed in the fiercely competitive environment of today's music industry.

In Part Two, "The Hit Formula," we'll expand our perspective to look at what makes a hit song work its magic, finding the balance between surprise and familiarity, form and substance, timeless emotion and up-to-the minute fashion. The formulas for successful songwriting are as old as Leiber & Stoller and Motown, and as fresh as today's Top 10. As much as popular music styles may change, the recipes for a hit remain as constant as the foundations of music itself.

Finally, in Part Three, "Write Your Own Hit," we'll bring a hit-maker's perspective to the fundamental elements of songwriting: melody, rhythm, lyrics, and the all-important "hook." It's not enough to understand what a hit song is, or even how one is made. Sooner or later, you want to write one for yourself—or to reinvestigate one of your existing songs and maximize its hit potential. Creating a song that can climb the charts, and maybe even become a classic, means testing and refining each element until it meets the highest creative standard.

Throughout this book, you'll find "Inside Track" profiles of industry movers and shakers. Here, we'll identify and articulate the qualities that influence A&R people, managers, radio programmers, producers, and promotion executives to give a song the all-important thumbs-up. "Gut instinct" is not an inherently irrational process, only an inarticulate one. I've challenged some of the most influential people in the business to discover what determines their immediate reaction to a song and then asked them to offer their own advice to aspiring songwriters.

This book will also guide you through specific exercises, the "Songwriter's Challenge," that you can apply to your own music. Taken together, this series of hands-on, proactive approaches aims to help you look at your work in a new light, inspire you to think and create in ways you haven't before, and transform a "good" song into a career-making record.

By now, you're either eagerly skipping ahead to chapter one, or you've got one last question: "Why all the emphasis on hits? Isn't it a rather narrow, overly commercial way to define success in songwriting? Surely, there is more to any artist than just the hit singles." Indeed, there is. But for those who wish to make their living in the music industry, hits are what matter.

Hits can accomplish what a thousand interesting, pleasant, or experimental album tracks cannot. Hits have *impact*! Only hits can transform an unknown artist into a worldwide celebrity almost overnight. Whether it's "Heartbreak Hotel" for Elvis Presley, or "I Wanna Hold Your Hand" for The Beatles, or "Sugar, We're Goin Down" for Fall Out Boy, nothing else can connect an artist to his or her audience like that one song that seizes the moment and galvanizes the public.

This matters more today than ever before. As the downloading phenomenon continues to accelerate the demise of the CD format, the music industry is in some sense reverting to its roots. Not since the early 1960s has the industry been as "single"-focused as it is today. The quirky, left-of-center "album cut" that once served to round out an artistic statement on a twelve-song CD is quickly becoming obsolete, now relegated to the lonely nether regions of the iTunes music store. As indicated by the growth in single-song downloads, the skyrocketing ringtone business, and the continued popularity of compilations like *Now That's What I Call Music,* it's clear that today's consumer is deciding on a song-by-song basis what music he or she wishes to buy.

An artist can no longer plan on establishing an identity across a ten-song concept album or through three years of touring around each small market in the country. A statement that establishes who the artist is, and why he or she matters, must be made in one song— a song strong enough to penetrate a competitive field that now includes every band on MySpace.com. The old saw about "You're only as good as your last hit" has never been as true as today.

Still, there is a better, and deeper, answer to the question, "Why all the emphasis on hits?" It goes right to the core of why a songwriter pursues the challenge of making music. Ultimately, a songwriter must decide what motivates his or her creativity. Is it a desire for personal expression? Or is it a desire to communicate? They are not the same thing.

Expression simply means saying what you have to say, in exactly the way you wish to say it. It's a desire that seems to motivate a large portion of today's artistic community, from amateur songwriters posting half-developed songs on file-sharing sites, to critically lauded underground acts that scrupulously avoid any tint of mainstream acceptance. By that definition, expression is an easily attainable goal, and utterly impossible to judge or critique. If you feel you've put across what you want to express, who am I to inform you otherwise? Only you can determine the success of your own personal expression.

However, if your goal is to communicate, you've taken on a much larger challenge. You've also attempted something that is considerably more objective. You may feel that you've communicated an idea or an emotion quite clearly. But in the end, someone else will be the judge. If I, the listener, don't understand what you're saying or relate to it, then the message was not communicated with success. Like beauty, communication is largely in the eye of the beholder, not the creator.

In the world of popular music, a hit is the ultimate symbol of successful communication. Miraculously, one song can touch millions of listeners with a message, an emotion, or a melody to remember. While not everyone aspires to communicate at this level, it's worth at least considering the value of the endeavor.

Certainly, one obvious value of a hit song's capacity to communicate lies in the financial rewards that mass appeal can offer, which are increasing all the time. With the power to reach people around the world, command a spot on radio playlists for years on end, and spawn videos, toys, tours, ringtones, and Broadway shows, hit songs continue to keep the larger music industry, which includes the music publishing and licensing businesses, alive and growing, even during a time of declining record sales. More important, songs that sell, and continue to sell, keep songwriters prospering, along with their families and heirs, decades after the original record first hit the airwaves.

As a songwriter or artist, your life can be changed by a hit song. It can bring fame and fortune and open career doors that would otherwise remain closed. But beyond all of that, a hit song can change the life of those who hear it. It could be the song that a couple remembers from the night they fell in love or that a future superstar sang at her first talent show. It might be the song that gave inspiration to a desperate man, when no one else could reach him.

Have you ever had a stranger ask what you do for a living? If you told them you were a songwriter, I can guess the response you received: "Really? Ever write anything I might have heard of?" As irritating as the question can be, particularly when the person asking hasn't turned on a radio in two decades, you can't escape the truth of it. The history of popular music will be told through hit songs. The legacy of an individual songwriter will be written in much the same way. Hits are the songs that reach across barriers, becoming part of the lives of thousands, or even millions, of strangers around the world. Hits communicate.

When I was a songwriter, my publisher would send me off to each recording session with one terse instruction: "Write a hit." It was a little daunting, and I seldom lived up to it. Still, it was the right advice. Now I'll throw down the same challenge to you. Here is your chance to create songs that launch careers, change lives, and leave a lasting mark on the world around us. That's a tall order. In the upcoming pages, let's see what it takes to make a hit in today's music industry.

Part One
How a Song Becomes a Hit

CHAPTER ONE

Desperately Seeking Singles

The A&R Perspective

Here's an old songwriter joke:

Did you hear the one about the blindfolded man identifying the animals at the zoo? The first animal he held in his hands was soft and furry and had what felt like two long ears on its head. "It's a bunny," he announced, triumphantly. The next animal was wet and slippery. "A fish," he declared. Then he was given a snake. "Hmm..." he said. "It's slick, and slimy, and has no ears. Must be an A&R guy."

For those songwriters whose interaction with record labels has been limited, it may be useful to explain that A&R refers to "Artist & Repertoire." The A&R executive is the person at the record company responsible for choosing which artists get signed and which songs get recorded. For songwriters still waiting on a return phone call from an A&R person, the preceding explanation might start to answer that nagging question, What does this guy actually do all day?

Like politicians and sports referees, record company A&R people get more than their share of abuse. Most of the criticism comes from the same songwriters and artists who, only months earlier, were desperately trying to get permission to send in their material and who now find their own career fortunes linked to the judgments of the man or woman behind the desk. At almost every record company, an A&R person is responsible for deciding which songs have the potential to be hits. Having had the job myself, I can assure you that it's never an easy task.

Because they walk the tightrope between unbridled creativity and corporate responsibility, A&R executives can be maddeningly opinionated, frustratingly indecisive, and utterly incomprehensible, all within one half-hour meeting. Comments like, "I need you to take it to the next level," or "Let me run it by a few people and I'll let you know what I think," can leave songwriters seething on the couch, as the A&R person rushes off to his or her lunch appointment.

Nevertheless, a songwriter, famous or unknown, cannot choose whether to work with A&R people any more than Pedro Martinez can choose to work with an umpire. Someone has to call the balls and strikes, and the hits and misses. The job of a song-writer is to learn to cooperate with A&R. If you do, you will find that the A&R role in the hit-making process is not only inescapable but sometimes invaluable. As is usually the case when it comes to the complexity of human interaction, the first step in building a relationship is empathy.

The songwriter's challenge is to try to comprehend the world from the A&R side of the desk. As you play your latest and great-est demo, how does the music sound to an industry executive's ears? Naturally, you're convinced that your song is a smash. That's why you're playing it. Perhaps you're right.

But here's a question to consider: Would you bet a million dollars on it?

This is the challenge facing an A&R executive, each time he or she hears a song. Picking a hit is a gamble that can put more than a million dollars at risk, along with professional reputations, job security, years of project development, and an artist's career. A record guy's life is not all comped seats and lunches at the Ivy. To call a song a hit is to stand at the edge of the high-diving board and prepare to take the plunge.

Moreover, to declare something a hit is to take that plunge with the knowledge that nine times out of ten, the pool is empty. A veteran music business executive once reminded me that an A&R person could say no to every demo that crossed his or her desk and only be wrong about 1 percent of the time. The truth of the record business is that the vast majority of releases fail to earn back even a reasonable fraction of their cost. It's the success of a few hits every year that pays for the failure of everything else.

We hope. In recent years, as album sales have dropped precipitously, the industry's fragile economic situation has raised the stakes for the song-selection process even higher. A&R professionals have less and less room to be wrong. In such an environment, is it any wonder that A&R people often rely inordinately on songwriters who have written hits in the past or on songs that sound like carbon copies of last week's chart topper?

When I first switched from being a songwriter to working as a music publisher and A&R person, many of my songwriting cronies were eager to know how things looked from the "dark" side. Unfortunately, the one observation most readily apparent from the

A&R vantage point was something almost impossible to communicate to another songwriter, even those with years of experience. What A&R people can see that songwriters cannot is the incredible rarity of a genuine hit song. A songwriter believes he or she writes one each week. An A&R person prays to hear one or two a year.

Much of the difficulty lies in language. When most aspiring songwriters use the word *hit*, they mean "a good song." When most successful, professional songwriters use the word *hit*, they mean a "really, really good song." When A&R people ask for a hit, they are talking about something else entirely.

Hits = Singles

When A&R people use the word *hit*, they're talking about "singles."

More precisely, they're talking about a "first single." This is the song that will be released to radio, roughly six weeks before an album is scheduled to appear in stores. For a new artist, this single will be the first announcement to the public of what he or she is all about. For an established artist, the single will offer a preview of the new album's artistic direction. Every promotional effort, public appearance, and publicity opportunity will shine the spotlight on this one song.

It has been ever thus. Almost from the birth of the music business, single songs have been the force driving the industry. Even with all of the technical innovations, changes in audio formats, and shifts in public tastes and buying patterns over the years, the single has endured as the fundamental vehicle for artist development. By and large, careers in the music business rise and fall on the strength of individual songs.

Of course, with the advent of long-playing records in the 1940s, the balance of power shifted somewhat. By the mid-sixties through the seventies, concept albums like *Sgt. Pepper's Lonely Hearts Club Band* or *Dark Side of the Moon* established the LP as the primary source of income for record companies, and by the late 1990s, many companies elected to quit selling singles altogether.

Yet, even this development failed to stem the industry's reliance on the hit song. After all, *Sgt. Pepper's* may not have had any singles released from it, but it certainly had its share of classic songs. *Pet Sounds* was defined by "Sloop John B." and "Wouldn't It Be Nice." Even an alternative act like Nirvana needed "Smells Like Teen Spirit" to propel it to superstardom. Albums may have been the industry's greatest source of income, but it took hit singles to sell them.

It still does. In fact, with the rise in song-by-song download-ing, it's clear that the audience's appetite for hit singles is growing, not declining. Fewer listeners are interested in digesting a twelve-song artistic statement from an individual artist. Instead, they are seeking out single songs, just as Top 40 radio listeners have been doing for decades.

Is it any wonder then that A&R people have little patience for "really, really good songs"? That's not what they need. They're desperately seeking singles. The sooner songwriters figure out the difference between the two, the sooner they can begin to supply what the music business needs.

What Makes a Single?

On the one hand, a hit can be hard to define. On the other hand, a single has very particular characteristics and fills a very specific function, making it much easier to describe. When you substitute the word *single* for the word *hit*, it's not so hard to understand what those in A&R positions are looking for. What makes a song a single, from an A&R perspective?

Singles Are Up-Tempo

Not always, of course. "Yesterday" was a pretty big hit. But when it comes to the "first single"—that leadoff release that sets up all the subsequent singles for success, including the soft, sensitive ballads—A&R departments want tempo, and plenty of it.

It's a matter of mathematics. Whether it's pop, rock, country, or urban music, most radio stations will play three or four up-tempo or mid-tempo records for every one ballad. After all, radio is entertainment, and entertainment needs pacing. Two consecutive slow songs will sap the energy from a show, and listeners will reach for the dial. Three ballads in a row will have drowsy drivers across the city careening into each other. People tune in to the radio looking for a good time, and for radio this means energy, fun, and tempo.

For a record company, this creates a very simple equation. You are three times more likely to get an up-tempo song on the radio than a ballad. If you're trying to write a song that will get airplay, set your metronome somewhere above ninety beats per minute (bpm) and go from there.

Okay, okay. It's not quite that simple. Sometimes, the difference between an up-tempo song and a ballad is more a matter of "feel" than actual beats per minute. This is especially true with hip-hop. "In Da Club" by 50 Cent is roughly ninety bpm on the metronome. Yet, no one would mistake it for a ballad. The feel, level of aggressiveness, lyrical approach, and energy immediately establish the song as an up-tempo record. People dance to it in clubs, blast it from car stereos, and bounce to it in their rides. This doesn't happen with ballads. It's not hard to tell the difference.

The true test is simply this: Will it add energy to a radio show or pull it down? A first single needs every possible advantage. Tempo is an edge you can't afford to forfeit.

Singles Fit the Format

Tempo is only one of the considerations when it comes to picking singles that will work at radio. Every radio station adheres to a very specific model, designed to appeal to a carefully targeted audience. If the point of a single is to get on the radio, then most of the time it pays to take the path of least resistance. This means giving each radio station a record that fits into its specific programming format. It means playing by the rules.

Rules rarely sit well with creative people. So if it makes you feel better, think of the following radio rules like lines on a tennis court. The best players play the game very close to the edge. But if you want to be in the game, you have to play within the lines. When it comes to singles, certain rules are all but inviolable.

LENGTH: Singles are under four and a half minutes. If your hit is over 4:45 seconds, you need to edit it. If you don't, someone else will. If the song can't be cut down to size, then it's not a hit. No radio station will play it.

STANDARDS OF DECENCY: It's true—there aren't many taboos left. Still, depending on the format, you have to be aware of the language, messages, and subjects that are acceptable. You can get away with a lot more cursing in hip-hop than in the world of adult contemporary. As the Dixie Chicks have learned, certain political messages can be deadly in country music. The question is not whether something is offensive, but rather whether it will offend the specific target audience. Artists ranging from Prince to Loretta Lynn have pushed right up to the boundaries of taste and social acceptability. Nevertheless, no A&R person will be interested in a song that crosses over that line.

STYLE: Listen to the radio, identify the format of the station you believe would play your music, and tailor your hit to appeal directly to that specific audience.

Don't fight the format.

That means rock songs must rock—and should not combine some country influences and a little bit of hip-hop with a soft, folky introduction. It means urban songs must appeal directly to the core street-level audience and should not require the support of pop radio to connect.

Aside from some college stations manned by sleepy-voiced musicologists eager to follow Howlin' Wolf with Wolfmother followed by Wolfgang Mozart, most radio stations serve a very narrow audience, with a very narrow selection of music.

As maligned as they often are, radio formats do everyone in the music business a very big favor. They allow artists, record companies, and songwriters to directly target the audience they are trying to reach, without wasting a great deal of time, effort, and money on those who will never react to a particular artist's work. If every station played all types of music, it would be almost impossible to break a new artist in any significant way. No record label would ever be able to build a critical mass of support among a core audience, without promoting every record to every station all of the time.

A couple of years ago, I was at an A&R meeting where one executive presented a new project for which he had high hopes, explaining that the artist, a young black woman, combined both rock and urban. There were hip-hop beats on the record, but she definitely wasn't an urban artist. The lyrics had a rock attitude, and some songs had some heavy guitars, but she wasn't really a rock artist either.

The room fell awkwardly silent. Finally, the president of the company broke in. "I don't get it," he said bluntly. "Who *is* the audience then? Where do we take this? What radio station? What are we going to do with it?"

This is not the reaction any A&R person is looking for. In fact, the artist was dropped from the label roster a month later, before the record was ever released. The phrase in the business is "falling through the cracks." It's a lonely place to be.

Singles Are Identifiable

I love this scenario. A songwriter comes in with a rough demo, eager to play Mr. A&R Guy the smash hit written only hours ago. "Can't wait to hear it," says Mr. A&R Guy, visions of a promotion to senior vice president dancing in his head. "What's the title?"

"We're not sure yet. We've got a couple of ideas. We just need to narrow it down," the songwriter replies.

Huh? Is there not one line that repeats? Is there no part of the chorus that sums up everything that's come before in one memorable phrase? Is there a chorus at all?

> # If you aren't sure of the title, or can't remember it, you don't have a single.

The hit "Ridin'" by Chamillionaire repeats the phrase "ridin' dirty" ten times in one chorus (I counted). "You're Beautiful" by James Blunt repeats the phrase three times at the beginning of every chorus. Even rock songs, which tend to use repetition less than most other styles, usually try to lock in a phrase that's striking enough to set the song apart. If you, the writer, don't know what to call the song, neither will Mr. A&R Guy. But you can be sure that he won't call it a single.

Singles Are Timely

Many of the most timeless hits in popular music were in fact written as a very direct expression of their time. Hendrix's "Purple Haze" is an enduring classic, but it emerges from a very specific historical and social setting. What could be a more perfect depiction of the Swing Era than "In the Mood"? Could anything but the seventies have inspired "Stayin' Alive"? This is the accidental genius of pop culture. Things created to capture a moment wind up lasting for generations.

It's easy to look at the Hot 100 and find songs that clearly reflect the social fashions, trends, and products of the moment. Hip-hop artists, writers, and producers are perhaps the most effective at this, continually dropping references to popular products or current events, sneaking in a new bit of slang, and mixing and remixing their tracks to ensure that the beats are hot and contemporary.

Yet even artists in a supposedly "untrendy" market like country find themselves frequently changing with the times. In 2002, Faith Hill released the song "Cry," written by a New York–based rock writer, Angie Aparo, and produced by Marti Frederiksen, best known for his work with Aerosmith. It was about as "pop" as any country artist ever sought to go. Three years later, the first single off Faith's new album was "Mississippi Girl," with the lyric "A Mississippi girl don't change her ways..." Something sure changed. What was it? The political climate had grown more conservative. Audiences had grown weary of the glitzy teen pop phenoms who ruled the airwaves at the beginning of the century. From a personal career standpoint, Faith needed to reconnect with her core country audience. The single choice was influenced by all of those factors.

Singles Define Artists

We've already noted that hit singles are often strongly linked to the times in which they become popular. They are also inextricably connected to the person who sings them—and this is the most important consideration for an A&R executive.

As important as a hit single is, it remains a means to an end. For the record executive, the ultimate prize is the creation of a hit artist. As we'll discuss in chapter three, the true function of a successful single is to be the catalyst that sets all of the marketing wheels in motion. Almost every well-known musical artist is linked to the success of one single song, which put that artist on the public map.

Before the release of her first single, Britney Spears was a complete unknown, an undefined teenage girl. Within weeks after the release of "...Baby One More Time," she was a worldwide celebrity, whose vocal sound and public persona were inextricably linked to that first smash hit. This is how powerfully one hit song can define an artist.

Around the same time, Christina Aguilera had a similar experience. Her first single, "Genie in a Bottle," and the follow-up, "What a Girl Wants," established her as a similarly sexy, young, dance-oriented artist with an attitude. Unfortunately, a problem quickly emerged. Christina Aguilera didn't want to be this kind of artist.

Christina called her follow-up album *Stripped*, because, as she put it, she was interested in "stripping all the elements I felt weren't me on that [first] record away." Yet, it was only when she released an equally significant hit song, "Beautiful," that she was able to reposition herself in the public eye effectively. A musical artist can't define or redefine her- or himself through videos, interviews, or album cuts alone. Only a hit single can create the picture, and only another hit single can alter that picture.

It's not surprising then that A&R people are so careful in their choice of the album's first single. It's not enough for the song to be up-tempo or identifiable, or just generally catchy. It's not even sufficient that it's timely and a perfect fit for the radio format.

To define an artist to the audience, an effective single has to offer the perfect summary of the artist's identity. If the song doesn't sound like something the artist would say, doesn't match up musically to the direction the artist is going, doesn't show off the best features of the artist's voice, or doesn't establish the artist as a unique individual, then it's probably not a single.

Wow. That's a lot of variables. It's also not surprising then that singles are so hard for record companies to find or for writers to dream up. The wonder is that it happens at all. For most professional songwriters, it doesn't happen by accident. Every element of a single is consciously crafted to reinforce the persona of the artist and to communicate his or her message.

In this respect, a good songwriter is not unlike a screenwriter. A potent film script doesn't just tell a story; it also establishes memorable, fully fleshed characters. Similarly, a song must create, or at least reinforce, a persona for the person singing it. Songs can accomplish this lyrically, through subject matter ("California Girls" or "Sweet Home Alabama"), the use of language ("Nuthin' But a 'G' Thang" or "Hollaback Girl"), or the message of the lyric ("Born in the USA" or "Imagine"). They can also create character through key musical elements—think of the amusement park organ on "California Girls" or the saxophone melody that opens Sade's "Smooth Operator."

When characters in a movie are well written, the process of definition is almost invisible to the audience. Most likely, there's no narrator to explain who each person is. Nor do the characters themselves tell the audience what kind of people they are. The audience gathers the information intuitively from everything they see and hear—the dialogue, the action, the gestures, and the plot.

Similarly, when a song works well, the singer is defined on every level at once. If you've heard "Satisfaction," you understand the Rolling Stones. You know their attitude, their musical style, and their whole way of looking at the world. It's all communicated in three minutes and twenty seconds.

Turning Songs into Singles
Steve Lunt

ATLANTIC RECORDS A&R

When it comes to finding that artist-defining first single, no one is more aware of the challenge, and the high stakes involved, than Steve Lunt, vice president of A&R at Atlantic Records. Steve is both an accomplished songwriter, with hits like Cyndi Lauper's "She Bop" to his credit, and one of pop music's most successful A&R executives, with a track record that includes Britney Spears, *NSYNC, Backstreet Boys, and Aaron Carter.

STEVE LUNT: The best advice any writer could get is this: Learn how to write a commercial, different-sounding, up-tempo record. It's the hardest thing to do, and it's the thing that every single A&R person on the planet is after. You need a lyrical concept that makes an up-tempo song something that an A&R person is proud to play to the president of the label, as being creative and commercial at the same time.

Right now, the biggest mistake I see writers make is that when you ask them for an up-tempo song, they have no imagination with the lyrical concept. Everything is about "Hey, Mr. DJ" or some southern expression for shaking your butt on the dance floor. It's so generic. Why can't writers apply the same imagination to the lyric on an up-tempo song that they would to a mid-tempo or a ballad?

What really taught me this was my success with "She Bop"—I have Cyndi Lauper to thank. I had this song sitting around with a pretty risky subject matter. I thought it was going to forever stay on my shelf until she came around and heard it and said, "Perfect. Let's do it." I suddenly realized, as long as you frame it in the right way, and don't make it offensive, you can actually write a song about anything you want. All the great writers—they're not afraid to go for something. If it's got soul and style, and a good melody, then the fact that the lyric is different works in the song's favor.

For an A&R person, the bottom line is that you can't fake a hit. It's as easy as that. When it's the real thing, you don't sit around discussing it. If you have to sit around and discuss it, and play it for ten people to work out if it's a hit—chances are, it's not a hit. With a genuine hit song, you know it immediately, and you can't stop it once it's out.

While A&R people may pick the singles, they alone can't turn those songs into hits. Indeed, no one in the music business can. Even after winning over the record company with an up-tempo song perfectly suited to the radio format and the artist, a songwriter needs the support of decision makers in an entirely different industry before a song can become a hit. So next, let's meet the people with the ultimate power to make or break your music.

CHAPTER TWO

Radio Rules

Putting a Song into Play

For most songwriters, radio is the spark that lit the flame. The dream of hearing your song on the airwaves is often the initial impetus to pick up a guitar, or a paper and pen, and begin the quest to become a songwriter. Unfortunately, many songwriters' knowledge of how radio works begins and ends with that initial dream.

Despite the crucial role that radio plays in bringing music to the attention of a mass audience, few songwriters understand much about the radio business. Who picks the songs that get played? How do they decide? Even more important, what can you do to make your song more "radio friendly"? This is the information a songwriter needs to navigate from that early vision of "What if that were my song on this station…?" to the reality of Top 40 success. The first challenge is to understand the strange, and often strained, union between radio and the music industry.

Think of it as a typical Hollywood marriage. What begins as a mutually beneficial union of convenience quickly progresses into a strained business partnership of not-so-equals and eventually winds up splashed across the tabloids, mired in scandal and recrimination. Such is the relationship of radio and records.

And yet, it endures. Even in the iPod and Internet generation, radio remains the primary spot where the public discovers new music. Going all the way back to the 1930s, radio has weathered all challenges of payola scandals, television, MTV, corporate consolidation, and an increasingly fragmented market to emerge bloodied but victorious, still clutching the role of the ultimate hit maker.

Although record executives may be loath to admit it, the people who really make the hits are not those in the corner office at label headquarters. The true hit makers are the radio programmers.

Those with the last word on whether to expose or dispose of a record are radio's music directors (MDs), who decide each week which forty to fifty songs will be cycled around the playlist of your favorite station. Despite all the criticisms leveled at radio from the music industry—playlists that are too tight, a recurring failure to announce the artists or song titles, too much talk, too much testing, too many shady deals—it is almost impossible to break a new artist into the commercial mainstream without the support of radio.

Television can break a song or artist faster, but it does so far less often. A relentless regimen of touring and album releases can also do it, but much more slowly and at far greater expense. MySpace, YouTube, and all of the Internet outlets have yet to show that they can do it at any level beyond that of a month-long novelty. In the end, if you want your song to be a hit, it needs to be on the radio. If you ever wondered how the Top 40 station in Cleveland gets all those superstars to come and perform at the annual Snowball Party in the dead of winter, you now have your answer.

Complain as they might, record companies are well aware of the power radio wields. Seldom does a label select a single without having first surveyed the opinions of the radio promotion department. Rarely is a judgment rendered by the promotion staff without a formal or informal poll of a few key MDs in that particular format. Then, once a single is picked, a label expends prodigious amounts of money and effort on persuading radio stations to play it. It may cost up to $500,000 to break a new song onto the playlists of the key stations across the country. This pays for prize giveaways for station listeners, artist "meet and greet" tours at stations around the country, advertising buys, and those various other vaguely defined "promotional" expenses that show up in expense reports and government investigations.

All of this care and feeding buys the one thing that no other medium can offer: the chance to reach a carefully targeted nationwide audience and to expose those listeners to a song over and over again. The power of radio is built on R&R, and I don't mean rock 'n' roll. I mean: rotation and research.

Rotation—Go Back Jack, and Do It Again...

"How many times do I have to hear this song? That's the problem with radio. They just play the same songs over and over again..."

I know. We've all said it. In fact, songwriters say it more than anyone. "Why must we be constantly subjected to the same thirty songs?" we complain.

Unless one of those thirty songs is ours.

Then of course, we wonder why the station has to play those other twenty-nine records. After all, the first time that Elvis showed up on radio, Memphis DJ Dewey Phillips played "That's All Right Mama" eleven times in a row. Look what it did for Elvis.

As songwriters, repetition is our friend. Sure, eleven times in a row on one song is a little much. But much of radio's hit-making power derives from rotation. No one plays a record once. Records are placed in rotation. It's like Grandpa's funny stories—if you miss one the first time, just wait an hour and it will come around again. By the third time, you'll remember it.

Radio can afford to be repetitive because of the nature of radio listening. Most people listen to the radio in relatively short stints throughout the day. That means that most listeners will hear only four or five songs out of a playlist of thirty songs in any given listening period.

Therefore, a radio programmer has one simple objective. He or she has to make sure that whatever four or five songs you catch during your listening minutes perfectly communicate the image and appeal of the station. This means coming up with a narrow list of song selections and sticking with it throughout the day. There may be some concessions to the hour, with a slightly softer appeal in the morning, and the heavier stuff pushed into the night. But in general, the MD is hosting a party that goes on all day long. It has to be rockin' no matter when you walk in the room.

Despite songwriters' griping, repetition is actually commercial radio programming's greatest contribution to the music industry. In fact, the difficulty with satellite radio, which seeks to offer a more eclectic alternative to traditional radio, is the diversity of the playlists. It's very hard to break a new artist, or even a new record, on these stations. No one song is played often enough to reach a mass of listeners—certainly not often enough to stick in the head of those who hear it.

Very few songs are so catchy that one listen alone can imprint the song indelibly on our brains. In most cases, the first listen captures our attention—we can make up our minds whether or not we'd like to hear the song again. At best, we might remember the title and one or two key elements. Only with repetition do we begin to know a song well enough to sing along or to make a decision to buy it for ourselves.

This is why television, despite its power to reach millions of viewers with one performance, creates far fewer hit songs than radio. More often than not, television exposes a song once, and then maybe broadcasts a rerun several months later. Coupled with consistent radio play, that television performance can be a galvanizing event that drives listener interest and sales. Ricky Martin's performance of "Livin' la Vida Loca" on the Grammy Awards would be one famous example. Still, without radio airplay, one isolated appearance of a song on television is unlikely to ignite listener interest. Exposure is not enough. Repetition is the key.

For the songwriter then, radio's reliance on rotation is a double-edged sword. The same thing that makes hit records possible is what makes those radio playlists so difficult to penetrate.

The key is in understanding how a tightly formatted rotation affects which songs are chosen for a shot at radio success. There are two primary questions that determine whether rotation works for or against your song.

Does Your Song Fit the Format?

If you're trying to join an exclusive club, one good rule of thumb is not to show up in shorts at the black-tie dinner. Radio is nothing if not an exclusive club. Much of the success of your song at radio will rest on how well the song fits in at a particular station or in a particular format.

That doesn't mean that the song has to be a carbon copy of something else on the station. In fact, carbon copies present their own programming challenges. Why take a known hit out of rotation to make room for an unknown song that sounds like a clone? And what will a long sequence of sound-alike records do to a station's energy and the interest it generates? Copying is not the same as conforming.

But when it comes to radio, a certain amount of accommodation is required. If you write a beautiful ballad with a pan-flute solo in the intro and send it to rhythm radio stations that are all about tempo and energy, the song will not fit into the musical mix. If you write a song for a soft, adult contemporary (AC)–type artist, but stick a rap section in the middle, the only rotation you'll see is your CD flying like a Frisbee out of the programmer's office.

Every radio format projects a carefully calibrated musical identity and corresponding lifestyle brand. I once had a beginning songwriter send me a country song with a clear drug reference in the title. A successful country writer would know immediately that contemporary country radio is far too conservative to play a record that mentions anything beyond a little old-fashioned, Friday night drinking. Most country stations try to present a family-oriented image, by choosing songs that convey traditional, conservative values. A song that goes against the grain will not support the identity of the station, nor will it blend in with the other records aired on either side of it. Whatever qualities the song may have, it's not a hit in that format.

Even when sales numbers or listener requests attest to a song's popularity, it is almost impossible to persuade an MD to add a record that is at odds with the format of the station. Whether it's a lyrical message that clashes with an audience's values, instrumentation or tempo that doesn't blend with other records in the format, or a musical element that would jar a listener (like a rap in an AC song), anything that violates a station's identity will quickly disqualify a song for consideration at radio. The whole point of rotating records from a tightly controlled playlist is to ensure that the image of the station, its "vibe," remains consistent 100 percent of the time.

Does Your Song Bear Repeating?

The good news is that if your song actually makes it into a radio station's rotation, you'll hear it over and over again. The bad news is that you may soon find yourself getting as sick of your own song as you are of others. Sometimes there's a thin line between "catchy" and "irritating."

For instance, one of the difficulties of having a hit with a "novelty" song—one that reflects the current news, a parody, or just a gimmick (anything from Weird Al to the "Chicken Noodle Soup" song)—is that such songs tend to have a very short lifespan. Initially, they seem made for surefire commercial success: They're simple, instantly memorable, and good fun. But after a week or two in rotation, the joke wears out. If you follow a song like this on the *Billboard* chart, you will usually find a fairly impressive first two weeks, followed by an immediate drop, like Wile E. Coyote off a cliff.

Songs that bear repeating are a bit subtler. Of course, they retain an immediate appeal and a catchy chorus. But as we'll discuss further in chapter six, songs that stick around a while are carefully constructed to engage the listener on several different levels. There's not just one novel surprise in the chorus—there's one interesting idea in each section of the song. There's not only a strong melody, but there are also memorable elements in the musical arrangement. Most important, there's a lyric idea that is not only clever but also strikes a genuine emotional chord.

Radio stations measure everything, and one of the most important things they measure on each record is "burn." As you might guess, burn indicates audience fatigue with a particular song—too much burn, and the song goes out of rotation. Clearly, a certain amount of burn is inevitable. The more play a record receives, the more likely it is to burn out. Still, some records burn out much more quickly than others. A song that can withstand months of heavy airplay is one in which a listener can discover something new, even after repeated listens.

Which leads us to the second pillar on which commercial radio is based.

Research: Running Numbers

As you've probably already gathered from the brief discussion of the "burn" factor, radio programming is not a simple science. Long gone are the days that individual disc jockeys followed a gut instinct and played a song by a Memphis truck driver eleven times in a row. In the current media environment, where corporations like Clear Channel own a network of stations across the country, most local music directors are afforded very little freedom to choose what records to play. Those decisions are made on a national and regional level and then passed down to the local stations to ensure consistency and accuracy in reaching the target audience.

If you're thinking that leaves little room for creativity or inspiration, then you've read correctly. I once had a music teacher who liked to say, "Making music is an art, not a science." It could also be said, at least at the present time, that programming music for radio is a science, not an art. That's because radio is not about music. Radio is about advertising.

If there is a root cause of the dysfunctional marriage between the radio and record industry, it is the music industry's failure to comprehend the role that music plays in the life of radio. Record executives, artists, and songwriters tend to think that because radio

has the capability to expose new music, radio then has a corresponding responsibility to open slots on the playlist, back-announce, and
support new artists. It's a nice thought, but it's wrong. Radio has no
particular need or obligation to support the music industry.

For those in radio, music is just one of many different ways to
entertain and attract listeners. In that respect, music is no more or
less important than news, talk, traffic reports, sports broadcasts, or
call-in advice to the lovelorn. It is simply another kind of bait that
is used to draw an audience to a particular station.

Radio's real commitment is to the advertising community,
which actually keeps the station profitable. To succeed, a radio
station must attract an audience that is at once big enough to be
attractive to advertisers, specific enough to target accurately, and
at least affluent enough to buy what advertisers are selling. Then
the station must hold on to that audience.

This is where research comes in. Research permeates every
aspect of the radio game. Stations research their audience, they
research their own relationship to that audience, and they research
every aspect of their programming to see how it appeals to their
audience. To attract advertisers, radio must know every detail
about who's listening to the station—the audience's age, gender,
location, race, and spending power. To reach that specific market
effectively, radio needs to understand the lifestyles, likes and dis-
likes, aspirations, and fears of their listeners. Finally, to keep their
share of the market, radio must follow how their listeners are
changing on a daily basis. What do they like today that they
weren't so sure about yesterday? Which celebrities did they once
think were "hot" but now label "over"? Which car are they trading

in and which one are they buying? What once favorite hobby do they now find boring?

The answer to all of this is research, research, research.

Just as radio's focus on rotation can be both a boon and bane to the songwriter, radio's reliance on research cuts both ways for the creative community. Much of the unique power of radio lies in its ability to target a very specific audience with pinpoint precision. This is made possible by research. Likewise, research gives the actual audience the last word—it removes the biases, prejudices, or just blind ignorance of any one particular programmer. The chances of one MD being wrong about your song are probably fifty-fifty. The chances that three weeks worth of audience research could also be wrong are considerably less.

On the other hand, the relentless rigors of the research process can leave a songwriter feeling like a cross between a lab rat and a circus animal. It starts with a call from the A&R person or a friend in the radio promotion department, offering breathless reports of initial testing numbers that are "over the moon," and confident predictions of a Top 10 smash. Two weeks later, the phone is eerily quiet. A careful reading of the charts indicates the song is failing to pick up adds (commitments from station MDs to work the song onto their playlists) in key markets. "The call-out research doesn't look so good," admits your inside source. "We're starting to lose spins. But don't worry—next week we're sending out a new remix that tested great in the Northeast..." No sooner has your song made the leap through one hoop of fire than another hoop appears, and another after that. Indeed, the testing never ends. It's a Finals Week that just keeps going.

In fact, the research on a song begins even before the record label delivers it to the radio station. With over a million dollars at stake, a record company needs to know before choosing a single what the audience reaction might be to a particular song. For almost all major labels, research is now part of the record-making process, just as it is part of the movie business and the television world as well.

Most record labels employ independent consulting firms to test a song being considered as a single, by playing it for Internet-based focus groups or by auditioning it to groups of listeners gathered in a room. The song will be played, usually in its entirety, and listeners will be asked to provide their reaction:

- Did they love it?
- Did they like it?
- Did they not care?
- Did they not like it much?
- Did they hate it?

This largely mirrors the testing that will be done by radio, once the single is selected by the label. That similarity is intentional. Labels often use the results of this initial testing to persuade radio to give a song a try. The label tests can also expose problems in the radio testing process, should there later be a major discrepancy between the label's results and those of an individual radio station. But most important, this initial testing tells the label the chances of a song's success and alerts them to problems that need to be fixed before the record enters the real competition.

The first round of actual radio testing occurs after an MD agrees to give a song an opportunity to find its way onto the playlist. Anything that doesn't meet the MD's initial approval can probably be declared DOA. Only once that magical combination of label pressure, promo guy glad-handing, and favor-swapping has placed a song into "testing" does the real fun begin.

Ideally, a song will be given at least one hundred spins (plays on the station, or stations) before radio begins testing its audience. During this time, a song might start to gather some audience awareness and, if all is going well, trigger some reaction in the form of "call-in" requests. As a kid, I was always calling my local station to ask them to play some obscure song I'd found on a decade-old album. Of course, they never did. But while stations might not fulfill requests, they do keep track of them. Generating "phones" (call-in requests or Internet requests) is an early indicator of a song's hit potential. Any song that can compel a listener to call or send a request is the kind of "reactive" record that labels and radio are looking for.

After approximately one hundred spins, the testing moves from "call-in" research to "call-out." Call-out research is the primary form of testing employed by radio to gauge listener response. This involves contacting a cross-section of listeners, through the phone, or more often, through the Internet, and rating their reaction to the song. The crucial differences between this kind of radio testing and the initial tests run by the record label are the amount of music played and the questions asked.

Unlike the record labels, radio tests records by playing their listeners "call-out hooks"—these are ten-second snippets, provided by the record company, of the song's hook. Then the listener is asked: Do you know this record?

At this point, the song has received spins on the station. Presumably, there is some kind of record label marketing campaign being waged as well. Hopefully, the song registers somewhere on the listener's radar screen.

Next, the listener is asked to register his or her reaction to the record, usually by selecting between several options that range from pure loathing to ecstatic embrace. In the last phase, songs are assigned favorability ratings. These ratings, which are continually readjusted, will determine the song's progression through light, medium, and heavy rotation—then back out again. As with SAT scores or your checking account balance, there's no evading the power of these numbers. For better or worse, they will determine the future of your song.

If you see a glaring problem in this process, you're not the only one. Sticking with the metaphor of a marriage to describe the relationship between radio and records, we can characterize the ten-second call-out hook as one of those pet peeves between partners that invariably leads to a knock-down, drag-out fight. Record companies hate the fact that million-dollar judgments are made by playing a listener less than a full chorus of a song. Radio points out that it's the labels who decide which ten seconds to test. For the songwriter, it all amounts to a high-stakes game, with the potential for big misunderstandings.

Needless to say, it's crucial that the record label pick the right ten seconds of the song to create the call-out hook. Stories abound of instances where the label's own testing, conducted by playing the whole song, yielded excellent results, while radio's subsequent call-out research came back negative. This usually indicates that the ten-second call-out hook is not the right section of the song's chorus. Not a tough problem to diagnose—but a very hard one to correct.

Unfortunately the testing period for a record is relatively short and getting shorter all the time. Most stations will give a record approximately six weeks from those initial spins to begin generating a positive reaction. If, two weeks into the process, the label discovers that the call-out hook is the wrong one, it will invariably take at least a week to correct it. By then, the record may be irreparably damaged. Round two of testing is one where many records meet an early, and sometimes unfair, end.

If a song survives the first two rings of research, it will begin to be worked into the rotation, based on its favorability rating. That's good news, but the game has only just begun. Records are continually monitored through call-out research to see if they are growing in popularity, stagnating, or "burning," and shifts are made in the rotation according to the research results. In addition, MDs closely monitor a song's performance in other markets and other radio formats to determine a record's long-term potential. Software programs like the Broadcast Data System (BDS) and Mediabase provide programmers with an up-to-the-minute report on when and where a song was played, how many times a day, and at what time of the day. All of these factors will determine how long or how deeply a radio station will commit to any particular song.

THE INSIDE TRACK

A Tough Game Getting Tougher
Hosh Gureli

HOSH G. LLC & MASTERBEAT.COM

As MD of San Francisco's legendary station KMEL in the late eighties and early nineties, Hosh Gureli, together with Program Director Keith Naftaly, laid the foundation of today's rhythm radio and crossover formats, breaking a wide variety of urban and club-based records into mainstream Top 40. Today, Hosh watches the changing radio industry from a different vantage point, as an independent A&R consultant. What he sees is a radio industry struggling to remain creative in a highly competitive business environment that increasingly demands immediate results.

HOSH GURELI: With the corporate consolidation, as well as some of the new technology like BDS and Soundscan, the window of time that a record has to surface as a hit is very small.

Records need time to marinate on radio. Some of the best records take a while to catch—they often become the ones that last forever. It might take more than a hundred plays. It might take 250 plays, but when they do catch, you find the burn is less. Right now, you only get about a hundred spins before a record goes into call-out research.

It used to be that research was used as a guide, to confirm what we felt. If something wasn't catching on, but we felt strongly about it, we kept it on the radio. Some of the best records, the classics, didn't go through the scrutiny that songs go through now.

When I worked at KMEL, we had what they called the "Brat Pack"—Michelle Santosuosso, Kevin McCabe, Al B. Dee, and myself. We'd find a record that we all loved, get on a conference call, and say, "Forget what the label's priorities are—we're gonna break this record." PM Dawn, Soul II Soul, C & C Music Factory all broke that way. We would go on a record, and stations around the country would follow like dominoes.

For an individual MD at a Top 40 or a Clear Channel station today, that would be very tough. You have to come in with so many facts and figures. In that sense, technology is the best and the worst. Today, it's such an exact science that it takes the feel out of it.

Survival Skills for the Radio Race

For most songwriters, a glimpse into the inner workings of radio can be terrifying. A co-writer of mine used to say that having a song released on an album was like sending your child out into the world. If that's the case, then having a song sent to radio is like leaving your child in the jungle for six weeks and hoping that when you come back you find him or her healthy and thriving amidst the wild beasts. With the intense pressure to fit the format, grab a coveted slot in the rotation, and produce positive research results, radio is a songwriter's survival test—and short of launching your own call-in campaign (it's been done), there's not much you can do once your song hits the airwaves.

Nevertheless, there are things you can do in the writing process to prepare your song for the odyssey it will one day face. The key to making it through the fiery rings of radio research is to be sure that your song is properly constructed, so that it can conquer the challenges it will encounter. Once you understand the process, it's not difficult to isolate the key elements that will carry a song through the tests that lie ahead.

Know Where You're Going

Target the exact radio format most likely to break your song. If you're not sure what radio formats exist (and there are many), check out *Radio & Records*, which is the weekly bible of the radio industry. It's easy to decide that your song is most likely to break on CHR (contemporary hit radio, or what used to be known as Top 40), but be aware that most labels avoid going directly to CHR stations with anything other than superstar artists. Most records have to build momentum in more specialized formats (urban, rhythm radio, country, hot AC, rock, modern rock, etc.) before they begin to generate interest at CHR. Try to find the format that will be the most open initially to your type of song.

The Songwriter's Challenge

Find the local radio station in the format you've identified, and try playing the demo of your song while you're listening to the station. How easily does it fit into the rotation? Does it match up to the other songs in the playlist? Does the energy rise or fall when your song comes on?

Analyze Your Audience

Radio's reliance on advertising requires that a programmer constantly be aware of the station's particular target audience—the exact demographic breakdown, changing tastes and interests, values, and opinions. It stands to reason then that the songwriter should have that same knowledge. You are never writing songs for a general audience. Whether you're writing urban, AC, country, or smooth jazz, you need to understand specifically who the audience for that particular music is. If you're song isn't relevant to that target market, it won't stand a chance at radio.

The Songwriter's Challenge

Do your own audience analysis. Start with some homework—read *Radio & Records*, *Hits*, or an advertising magazine like *Adweek* to get a clear idea of the demographics of the target audience you're trying to reach. Then take it a step further. What kinds of magazines does your target audience read? What TV shows do they watch? What are the hot fashions? Who are the celebrity trendsetters that your audience tends to follow?

Make the Hook Clear and Immediate

Remember that the call-out hook is ten seconds long. Try timing that out. On a mid-tempo song, it comes to about four measures, or in most cases, half the length of the chorus. If the hook is the first line of the chorus, then it's pretty easy to find the four bars that constitute the call-out hook. If the hook is at the end of the chorus, it can be a bit trickier. If you're not sure which part of the song is really the hook, then the record company may not be sure either. Remember, you want to aim for maximum impact and a minimum of confusion.

The Songwriter's Challenge

If someone asked you how your song went, what phrase of the chorus would you sing them? That's probably your call-out hook. If it doesn't reach out and grab you, then it's not a hook.

Do Your Own Testing

Radio tests. Record companies test. So why not songwriters?

Master P, the rap impresario, once explained to me that a key to his success was his ability to test his records at a grassroots level. Because he was so closely connected with his audience, he was able to take his music directly to a handful of hot clubs, mix-tape DJs, and taste-making kids in the community to find out immediately if a song worked for his market. By the time he went to radio, he had very little chance of failure—he had done all his testing already. That meant less risk for radio, less wasted promotion dollars for the label, and a track record of success that would build upon itself.

Of course, you can play your songs for your friends and family. Still, wouldn't it be better to play them for the actual audience to which they'll be marketed?

The Songwriter's Challenge

If you write rock songs, perform them yourself, or find a band to play them in a club. If you write dance music, meet some of your local DJs and ask them to give it a spin on Saturday night. Make friends at hair salons, restaurants, lounges, or clothing stores—anywhere the owner might be willing to put your CD on the sound system.

The only requirements are that the audience should match the target market for your song, the audience should not be entirely made up of your friends, and you should be there to watch the reactions.

Then notice:

How comfortably does your song flow into the mix of other music being played?

How did the crowd react? Which listeners reacted most favorably, or least favorably? Were there certain sections of the song that seemed to grab the audience's interest or lose it?

Let's Face the Music

Whether it's a casual test like those in this chapter's Songwriter's Challenges or the most sophisticated radio research, the goal remains the same: an objective, unforgiving reality check that will give a glimpse of a song's ultimate potential. This too often goes missing from the songwriting process.

It's easy to convince yourself that a song is "good enough" to be on the radio. But once you understand the rigors of the research process and the real factors involved in the hit-picking process, you have a much clearer sense of the challenges that lie ahead. Does your song appeal to the specific target audience of a particular radio format? Will it maintain and even increase its appeal after fifty spins in a week? Above all, will it grab a listener's attention with just a ten-second taste of the chorus?

"When you hear a number-one record, you know it," confirms Hosh Gureli. "They have that 'get outta my way' quality, as soon as they come on.

"The market is so cluttered, and the society is so cluttered today, that as an audience, we demand an immediate impact,"

Hosh explains. "A hit song has something special—it's different, but not too different. That's the formula the best writers know how to use."

That "get outta of my way" quality is our subject in chapter three. As Hosh points out, the ability to cut through the mass of music already in the marketplace is the ultimate challenge that faces every artist, record label, and songwriter, not only at radio but in every facet of the entertainment world.

The Challenge of Music Marketing

Cutting Through the Clutter

If you've ever sat in a meeting with a record label executive and sensed that your song didn't mean quite the same thing to him as it does to you, you were probably right. To a songwriter, a song is a blend of melody and lyric and harmony and rhythm, meant to communicate some kind of emotion or message. To the record label executive, a song is, first and foremost, a marketing tool. It is, in fact, potentially the greatest music marketing tool ever invented.

If that's the case, then any effective songwriter must learn to think, at least in part, with the mind of a marketer. This means that the work of songwriting begins long before any writing is actually done. You may think this subject has nothing to do with music. But the creative process begins by looking at the current market situation realistically, knowledgeably, and strategically.

Of course, no one in the record industry would ever discount the importance of melody, lyric, harmony, and rhythm in creating an appealing song. But in today's music marketplace, a song is much more than a three-minute slice of entertainment. A song is an essential weapon in a larger and more important campaign—the one that turns unknowns into stars, and stars into superstars.

Imagine yourself lost in the jungle, with only your trusty jungle knife to hack through the vines and branches and clear a path to safety. In the tangled web of our modern media culture, the song is the sword that cuts through the clutter.

It's not hard to figure out what the clutter is. Go to a record store and take a look around. Buy a music magazine and look at the new releases. Spend an evening, or perhaps a month of evenings, looking at new bands on MySpace. Or consider this:

At a recent SXSW, the annual Austin music conference dedicated to discovering new music, there were performances by more than a thousand bands.

We have met the clutter, and it is us.

As songwriters, singers, artists, band members, record producers, or label A&R people, we all contribute to the media and music clutter. In many ways, we are our own worst enemy. Often with the best of intentions, we overload the public with too much buzz, too much hype, and too much music for any normal person to absorb.

Unfortunately, the marketplace works on the same principle as your apartment. A little clutter only leads to more. When too much product begins to overwhelm the consumer, sales start to drop. Faced with the prospect of missing their profit targets, record labels respond to the falling sales figures by increasing the number of releases. After all, if you're selling half as many records, you'll need twice the amount of new product to make the year-end numbers. And with that, the whole vicious cycle begins again.

For the most part, there appears to be only one reliable solution to the problem of an overly cluttered marketplace: hits.

There is no quiet, subtle way for an artist to edge his or her way through the mass of releases. It's like trying to swim out of quicksand. You'll quickly be sucked under. Whether it's a hit song, a hit video, a hit media story, or a hit TV show, some kind of hit is usually the only force that will enable a songwriter, artist, band, or producer to break through and have his or her work register in the general public's consciousness.

This is the fundamental challenge of music marketing. What "hit" element will be the catalyst that enables a particular artist to break through the chaos of popular culture? Sometimes it may be a newsworthy or provocative public image—think Tiny Tim, Ice-T, or Paris Hilton. Sometimes it will be an iconic music video, like Duran Duran's "Girls on Film," Tone Loc's "Wild Thing," or "A Million Ways" by OK Go. These days, it could be an association with a hit TV show, the most obvious example being *American Idol*. Most often though, it will be a hit song that grabs attention at radio and then spurs actual sales. Whatever it is, there must be something to carve a path for the artist to move ahead, through the media jungle.

Not surprisingly then, the mandate to cut through the clutter is at the center of almost every issue that arises in the average day of a music marketing executive, artist manager, or record producer:

> Record Producer: How's the new mix?
> A&R Guy: Too subtle. It won't "break through" at radio.

Booking Agent: Can the band take an
opening slot on the tour?
Manager: It's not a fit for us. It won't grab
our active audience.

Marketing Director: Is this the first single?
Radio Promo Person: It's a good song, but
it's passive. Sounds like a turntable hit.

The subjects may change, but the debate remains the same. Since songwriters are so often in the middle of these fights (uh, I mean, "discussions"), but seldom present to watch the sparks fly, it's worth taking a quick look at the two most common battlegrounds in the world of music marketing.

The Great Debate: Passive or Reactive?

One dead giveaway to the fact that industry people don't look at songs in the same way as songwriters is the language that label executives use to describe music. Songwriters and artists are often baffled to hear their work labeled "passive." What does that mean? Is it bad or good?

Passive is not a musical term. It's a marketing expression, and it's the word used to describe most of the material that passes across a record executive's desk. *Passive* implies pleasant, unobjectionable, and generally agreeable.

Hmmm. That doesn't seem so bad, does it? It is. If you're trying to cut through the clutter, you don't want to be passive. A passive record is like one more of those little glass animal figurines on a shelf already full of them. It simply disappears among all the other ones just like it.

The key to music marketing is to find product that is "reactive." Reactive is surprising and controversial—possibly offensive or annoying—but sure to garner a response. When Frank Zappa first saw shock-rock act Alice Cooper at an L.A. club, the entire audience walked out on the performance. At the end, there were only five people left in the club, and four of them were in the band. The other person was Zappa. He signed the group to his record label on the spot. Zappa reasoned that most superstars engender almost as much hate as love, at least initially—Sinatra, Elvis, and The Beatles being just a few examples. If he'd found an act that some hated so vehemently, he assumed that he could find another audience who would love it.

In a crowded marketplace, it is easier to sell a product that triggers extreme responses than one most people merely tolerate. Reactive records get people talking; they generate their own publicity; they drive listeners to call the station; they make people want to be "fans." Reactive records have, quite literally, a life of their own. When it comes to music marketing, reactive beats passive every time.

Not surprisingly then, the great passive/reactive debate is reflected in every aspect of the industry. It affects entire genres of music—styles like ambient, lounge, or chill-out are, by their nature, generally passive, while hip-hop tends to be highly reactive. This is why there are a lot more platinum rap albums than chill-out albums and why major labels release many more hip-hop records than ambient tracks. Individual artists are deemed to be passive or reactive as well. Due in part to the generally safe and predictable material he has recorded, Nick Lachey remains a somewhat passive recording artist, and his uneven sales record proves it. On the other hand, ground-breaking, sometimes controversial singles like "Cry Me a River" and "SexyBack" have allowed Justin Timberlake to resurface after years of absence and rocket directly to the top of the charts. That's reactive.

When it gets down to individual songs, the discussion becomes even more complex. Some songs may be reactive at radio (at least enough to generate positive call-out research) but may not trigger big sales. These are called "turntable" hits. While they can be quite profitable for the songwriter (who gets paid each time the song is played on the radio), they are big money-losers for record companies. As I mentioned in the previous chapter, other songs may be highly reactive but burn very quickly.

It can be easy to classify songs or artists with a more reserved or subtle sound as passive and qualify all aggressive, up-tempo songs as reactive, but that's a dangerous oversimplification. Because of her quiet, laid-back sound, Norah Jones might appear to be the most passive of artists. In fact, her first week sales figures attest that she is strongly reactive to her core audience. Conversely, the charts abound with Green Day sound-alikes that despite plenty of aggression and energy fail to generate any overwhelming reaction to their music. A ballad like "I'm Already There" or "I Hope You Dance" may be far more reactive than a generic Southern hip-hop record. How hard a record tries matters much less than the results it achieves.

When it comes down to picking a single for any artist, the first question is very simple: Will this song get a reaction? Now of course, the second question is a bit trickier: Why?

The Great Divide: Falling Through the Cracks

Why do some songs that are corny, silly, and simplistic generate such strong reaction? Conversely, why do so many other songs, some of which are sophisticated, sensitive, and musically complex, float out into the vast sea of new releases and promptly sink like a stone, making barely a ripple on the surface before disappearing forever?

That's a tough one. Of course, there is more than one answer. If success has a thousand authors, then failure has a thousand explanations. But there is one primary reason why worthy songs, and worthy artists, often find themselves struggling to make an impact in the market:

> Like ships adrift on that sea
> of releases, songs are lost when
> they have no home.

As I discussed in chapter one, a song that has urban elements (but isn't really urban oriented) and rock elements (but isn't meant for a rock audience) doesn't belong anywhere. It has no demographic audience, no radio format, and no sales base to call home. Without that home, it is impossible to create a direction for a marketing campaign. Eventually, a song without a home will get lost in the crowd, drifting off into anonymity. It will fall through the cracks.

Have you ever lost something in the clutter on your desk? If it's something truly important to you, you'll tear up your entire work space to find it. But if it's something of mild interest, you'll probably look around for a few minutes and then promptly forget about it, until it turns up two years later in some secret crevice, covered with dust.

That's what happens when a song falls through the cracks. When a record matters enough to a core group of people, those fans will push through all the clutter to seek it out. On the other hand, if a record is of only passing interest, even to a very large group of people, no one will care enough to dig it out from all the other releases that month. Home is where people love and care about you—and every record needs a home. All success starts with a passionate core audience in one specific market.

This knowledge can be comforting to many young artists or developing bands. If you have a small but fiercely devoted fan base in your small town, don't be discouraged when you see other acts who have toured more widely or have a thousand more friends on their MySpace page. If your songs moved thirty people at the club to tears (this does not include your mother), don't agonize about the five who walked out early.

The most dangerous prospect for any music marketing strategy is to have a song that appeals a little to a lot of people. It's far safer to appeal a lot to a little group of people. A small, passionate audience creates momentum, which can then spread into other markets.

The key is to build a foundation on solid ground. If you do that, you can then construct a bridge from that point, to cross over to other audiences. But you can't raise a bridge by starting in the middle—there's nothing there to build upon. And it's a long, quick fall into oblivion.

The English have a saying that they use at the London Underground tube stops: "Mind the Gap." The rough translation is "Watch Your Step," and it's good advice in subway riding, and music marketing. Here's a quick map of some of the common danger zones, where songs go, never to be heard from again.

The Gap Between Pop and Urban

So many successful acts seem to live in this territory. Everyone from Justin Timberlake to Gwen Stefani to 50 Cent has managed to find homes at both urban and pop radio. Now, like the sirens of old, they beckon to aspiring artists to come join them in the best of all possible worlds…

Beware! It's a trap. The truth is, almost all of these artists started in one very specific genre, with songs that appealed directly and exclusively to that market. Justin Timberlake, as the lead singer for *NSYNC, sang pure pop songs for a pop audience. Gwen Stefani began as a rock artist, as part of No Doubt. 50 Cent made records directly aimed at the urban audience and then used

69

that momentum to move into mainstream pop radio. The rule of thumb is this:

First and foremost, any urban pop song must first be entirely credible as an urban record.

The crucial factor is the "musical track"—the chord progression, rhythmic groove, and the overall sonic quality. That's why pop-leaning artists like Gwen Stefani and Nelly Furtado employ hip-hop producers like Missy Elliott and Timbaland. If the track is aggressive enough to work in the urban market, a more pop-leaning melody and lyric may increase the song's ability to cross over. But if the track lacks the raw punch of a hip-hop record, no amount of "street" phrases or R&B inflections in the melody will make the song convincing.

The Gap Between Pop and Country

This one is slightly simpler to navigate than the urban/pop gap, simply because the crossover traffic generally runs in only one direction. There are quite a few country records that become popular enough to move onto the pop charts. But with the exception of a few ballads (Brian McKnight's "Back at One" or 98 Degrees' "I Do (Cherish You)," very few pop songs cross over to the country format. So:

If you want to write a country pop hit, you should start by writing a country hit.

Any successful country-pop artist, from Shania Twain to Rascal Flatts, must first establish themselves at country radio. This requires lyrics that resonate with a country audience, chord progressions that fit comfortably into the country style, and melodies simple enough to fit into the country tradition. A lyric that is too obscure or ambiguous (more Dylan than Hank Williams), music that is too harmonically adventurous, or a loose alt-rock type of song structure will send the song immediately into the Grand Canyon of failed crossover dreams.

The Gap Between Rock and Modern Rock and Punk and Pop

The rock market can be a little like a war zone. Unless you know your way around, you can easily find yourself stepping over some invisible boundary into enemy territory. With so many genres and subgenres, each with its own lifestyle, fashion, and media, you have to be very clear in deciding where you stand.

No good promoter puts an eye-shadow-wearing "emo" band on the bill for a jam-band festival. A band with a Top 40 radio hit will be instantly suspect to a hardcore punk crowd. In a market where credibility is the key to long-term success, the wrong drum sound, haircut, video production, or single choice can not only fail to cross a band over to a new audience, but it can instantly alienate the act's core following.

The Songwriter's Challenge

If you're writing a rock song for your own band, ask yourself: What acts could you open for on tour? The answer to that question should give a pretty clear idea of the exact market to which you're trying to appeal. Now picture yourself singing your new song in front of that type of audience. If you're not 100 percent comfortable, it's probably because you're falling through the cracks.

Especially in a market as fragmented as the current rock climate, you need a thorough understanding of your core audience. What other bands' T-shirts do your fans wear? What record labels do they regularly support? Who are their MySpace friends? Defining your market is not a matter of describing your own personal influences or interests. Songwriters and musicians often have unusually eclectic tastes. The definition of your target market is a precise description of the people to whom your music will appeal. Once you've narrowed that down, your lyrics, music, production, and imaging must aim directly at the center of the target, if you want to hit the bull's-eye.

The Space in the Crowd

Many songs, artists, and albums fall through the marketing cracks when they fail to identify the audience that should be their base—when they are unable to locate their "home." Others have a slightly different but related problem that renders them equally vulnerable: What if you know where your home is, but when you get there, nobody's around?

Not every audience is worth reaching. If you have concluded that your core market is fans of klezmer music, it will be very challenging to use that knowledge in the creation of a hit song. The cold, sad fact is that there simply aren't enough klezmer fans to serve as the basis for a genuine hit record. To attain a hit, you are going to have to identify a larger audience (perhaps the indie-alt-rock market) and try to make your music palatable to them.

Artists working in genres like techno, lounge, metal, classic AC, jazz, and Americana all face the same dilemma. Even if you release a song that appeals perfectly to the core audience, the fan base within those categories simply isn't large enough to build a superstar, or even one big hit. To write a hit metal song, you must make something that will move beyond the hardcore metal audience, into the rock mainstream. To create a jazz hit, you must write a song that not only appeals to a jazz audience, but an adult contemporary, or R&B crowd as well.

If you're in a very limited market, you must find a way to expand your music's reach into other genres to create a hit. All of the considerations that follow are at the forefront of the minds of the A&R staff, marketing department, and management team as they're listening to your song for the first time.

- Will it cut through the clutter?
- Will it generate a reaction?
- Is it a homerun for the core audience?
- Can it cross over to a larger audience?

As a New Yorker, I can tell you that the key to finding your way through a crowded, chaotic environment is to know the terrain and to have a plan. So before you pick up the guitar, or put pen to paper to start another song, it's worthwhile to look at what's already out there, and figure out how you might make your way through the traffic to get where you really want to go.

CHAPTER FOUR

The Solution to Music Marketing

Cracking the Code of Opportunity

It's easy to consider all of the challenges in music marketing—the clutter of the marketplace, the need for music that is reactive rather than passive, the danger of falling through the cracks—and come to the rather logical conclusion that the entire endeavor of creating a hit song is, well, impossible. From a statistical standpoint, the chances of breaking an unknown artist or launching a new single make playing the lottery look like a sound investment strategy.

Still, hits happen. Every week of every year, even during the worst of times in the industry, a new artist with a new song breaks out of the crowd, avoids the pitfalls, and somehow finds an audience, ready and waiting to crown him or her a star. The surprise is not that it happens at all, but rather how easily and quickly it can happen, despite all the odds against it.

This is the paradox of overnight success. Most industry veterans will assure you that such stories are preceded by years of hard struggle. Yet they will also acknowledge that once there's a hit song to drive the marketing campaign, the road from obscurity to superstardom can transform almost instantly from a rocky, uphill path to a straight shot on the open highway. Hits make it all look so easy. The question is: How?

The key lies in turning marketing challenges into opportunities. A sharp A&R person sees an overcrowded market and looks for a little piece of abandoned terrain where something different can take root. While passive songs get lost in the clutter, a savvy songwriter keeps things edgy enough to cut through, ensuring an audience reaction. In a sea of faceless artists searching for an identity, a smart lyricist provides not just a song but a story that will define an artist in one unforgettable chorus. Once those pieces are in place, cracking the code to chart-topping success can seem as simple as 1-2-3.

Step One: Find the Holes in the Market

Baseball's legendary Wee Willie Keeler said it best. When asked his secret of success at the plate, Wee Willie replied, "I hit 'em where they ain't." If you want to boost your "hit" average as a songwriter, you can start by taking a look at the field and finding the holes in the market.

As we've already noted, there are cracks in the market that are dangerous. The space between different genres is a no-man's land, and that's who you'll find there. It's hard to find a home for songs that fall between pop and urban, country and pop, or even between different subgenres of rock.

But there are other spaces in the marketplace, "holes" that are created when a particular segment of a genre's audience is not being properly served. These open spaces are the land of opportunity for the lucky songwriter who gets there first. Does every rock song on the radio sound like Coldplay? Then someone needs to write a swaggering, Bon Jovi–style rock anthem, for all those people in the market fed up with melancholy. Is the hip-hop market full of crunk-style party records? Then maybe it's time for something with a bit more of a social message, for the backpack kids that can't relate to Lil Jon.

In this particular endeavor, the lemming-like nature of the music industry works in your favor. In case you haven't noticed, most people in the record business are trend chasers. As soon as one type of sound finds success, the market is immediately flooded with sound-alike songs and sound-alike acts, all trying to appeal to the same group of people that liked the original hit.

When you can identify this situation in a market, it's time to call the marketing equivalent of football's "reverse" play. If everyone is running to the right, then hand the ball off to one guy running to the left. There'll be nothing but open field ahead. When every R&B

singer was trying to be as "hip-hop" as a rapper, John Legend went the opposite direction, making a sophisticated, romantic soul album. What he found was a vast worldwide audience that had been waiting in the shadows for just such a traditional R&B album.

Smart record labels, artist managers, producers, and songwriters always analyze their market and try to find the untapped audience within it.

The art is to read the field and get to the opening before anyone else.

The Songwriter's Challenge

Ask yourself:

1. What are the trends dominating your market at the moment? Which part of the audience is being served well by those trends? Which part of the audience is likely to be alienated by those trends?

2. What are the most common tempos of songs in your market? Can you come up with a song that differs markedly in tempo or rhythmic feel?

3. Are there types of songs that have worked for the market in the past but that are notably absent at the moment?

4. Are there lyrical subjects that are relevant to the market and not being addressed?

As long as you stay centered within a very specific genre or market (rock, pop, country, dance, hip-hop, etc.), you can be brave enough to go in a different direction than everyone else. That's where you'll identify the hole.

Step Two: Find the Edge

No single word (other than *no*) is more overused in the A&R person's vocabulary than the word "edgy." Everyone in the industry knows what it means, or at least thinks they do. It means provocative, surprising, controversial, timely, shocking, exciting. It is what most contemporary popular artists want to be.

You can't cut through an overgrown jungle with a dull knife. Because the record labels pump out so much product, the majority of which is generic and derivative, savvy artists continually strive to find an "edge" in everything they do. By putting an edge in their songs, their visual image, or their public persona, artists ensure that they will be the ones that the media talk about and an audience remembers.

Pressing buttons gets press.

All press is good press. Never shy away from a little controversy.

It's no surprise that successful songwriters know how to put an edge in their work, whether it's through provocative lyrical ideas or surprising musical elements. Legendary writer Billy Steinberg is a master of the edgy lyric, shown in classic hits such as "Like a Virgin" and "I Touch Myself." Both of these are very standard pop songs in their form and firmly settled within the mainstream pop genre. Yet, they also pack a little shock value in their hooks, which is exactly why they stand out.

In the same way, Michael Jackson's "Beat It," while not highly provocative lyrically, grabbed its audience on a musical level, because it combined the production values of pop and R&B with the aggressiveness of rock music to create an explosive new sound. In many ways, Justin Timberlake has brought us this generation's version of the same approach, blending provocative lyrics, like "SexyBack," with wildly inventive, unconventional tracks.

"Edgy" doesn't always have to mean "sexual" or "shocking." Sometimes, a very sincere, emotional approach can be very edgy, especially when a listener is expecting something else. Emo songs can be edgy, simply by the directness and vulnerability of the emotion.

Songs like Bruce Hornsby's "The Way It Is" or Tracy Chapman's "Fast Car" are edgy, because they confront uncomfortable social issues. Even Bob Carlisle's "Butterfly Kisses," in some ways the least edgy song ever written, is able to cut through precisely because the blatant sentimentality of the lyric goes so much against the grain of most contemporary pop songs.

The Songwriter's Challenge

More than anything else, finding your "edge" as a songwriter is about keeping your finger on the pulse of the times. As a songwriter, ask yourself:

1. What are the current topics or issues of controversy in society?

2. What can I do musically and sonically (in terms of production values) that will make my record immediately fresh and surprising?

3. How can I tell the story of each lyric with more attitude? Does the lyric put the singer in the position of being strong, defiant, and in control?

Step Three: Find the Story

An edgy lyric gives an artist a "story," which provides a critical tool in cutting through the clutter. A song with edge not only gets people talking, but it gives an artist something to talk about. When N.W.A. released "Straight Outta Compton" they didn't just break through the hip-hop market; they became a national news event. Suddenly, they had an identity, a message (of sorts), and a story for the press to grab onto.

Most of the time, the story starts with the song and the songwriter. The majority of artists begin the record-making process with an interesting voice, or a local following, or a good haircut, but not much actual identity. Even when the songwriter and artist are one and the same person, it is usually the songwriter side of the personality that must either discover the artist's story or, more often, invent one—and then create a song that establishes that narrative immediately in the listener's mind.

Did Johnny Cash really shoot a man just to watch him die— or was that just something from "Folsom Prison Blues"? Was Lynyrd Skynyrd really from Alabama? Is Eminem "Slim Shady" or is that just a character in a song? In the public's mind, there is very little difference. The song has provided a story, and now everything that follows, from wardrobe to video, will reinforce that image and attitude. A great songwriter begins by establishing a character for the artist, and then creates a song to reveal that character.

The Songwriter's Challenge

As every beginning journalist knows, there are five *W*'s that make up a story:

1. Who?

Whether you're writing for an artist, for yourself, or your own band, you need to put some thought into the character of the singer, before you start putting words in his or her mouth. What is this artist like? Is he or she young or old? Flamboyant or intro-spective? What is the artist's history and background? What does he or she look like?

2. What?

What is the artist about? What sub-jects interest him or her? What message would he or she want to send to the world? What does he or she do on a free Saturday night? What are the major influences, musical and personal, that shaped the artist?

3. When?

To what time period does the artist belong? No one is a product solely of the here and now. Prince was a symbol of the eighties, but much of his character was drawn from sixties stars like James Brown and Jimi Hendrix. The Scissor Sisters would feel perfectly at home in the seventies, the age of disco and glam rock. When artists want to reinvent themselves, they inevitably make up a new "when"—witness the transformation of Christina Aguilera into a forties-style chanteuse. History is always part of an artist's story.

4. Where?

To create a story, it helps to know where the artist is coming from, literally. Bruce Springsteen is from New Jersey. Who could imagine it any other way? The Eagles are from California, in every sense. Robbie Williams is as British as the Queen Mum. Many artists are inseparable from a very specific setting.

5. Why?

This is more challenging. "Why this artist?" "Why should we, the public, care?" The test is to identify the one or two qualities that make this particular artist noteworthy. Does the artist have an amazing, unique voice? Is there an important message in his or her lyrics? Does she have an irresistible personality? Until the "why" is answered, an artist's story is not complete.

Within the course of a songwriting career, you may often find yourself writing a song for an artist you have never met or about whom you have only limited knowledge. In that case, you'll do what any good journalist would do: research. Find out everything you can from the Internet, magazines, or television. If you still can't get the information you need, or if the information that you have is simply too dull to serve as the basis for a story, then do what any good novelist would do: Make something up.

Whatever your approach, try to avoid writing songs for an undefined "female pop singer," "male country artist," or "pop vocal group." Even if there is no specific artist to whom you think you have access, you still need to create an imaginary picture of a very specific character before you start to write a song. If you have only a vague idea of who might sing your song, you will inevitably write correspondingly vague lyrics and music.

This also applies to writing for yourself as an artist or writing for your own band. If you can't answer the Five W questions about yourself or your band, then your project has not yet matured to the point that it will be possible for you to write a breakthrough hit. If you can answer all of the questions, but none of the answers seems very interesting, you probably need to reinvent yourself and try to create a more compelling persona.

But if you can answer the Five W questions, and you find something in your answers that is unique, you can begin to build a marketing story for yourself as an artist. Your challenge as a song-writer will be to capture that story musically—not as autobiography necessarily (although it's been done), but as a statement of your artistic identity. "Like a Rolling Stone" didn't directly tell the story of Bob Dylan, but it certainly conveyed the essence of who he was as an artist, through both the music and the lyric. That's the challenge of songwriting: Done properly, it will be the catalyst of an effective marketing campaign. Done perfectly, it could make a marketing campaign almost unnecessary.

THE INSIDE TRACK

The Defining Hit
David Massey

PRESIDENT, MERCURY RECORDS

In his position as president of Mercury Records, David Massey is reestablishing a venerable label with a roster of new stars like Duffy, in a business climate as difficult as any in music industry history. Not only is he undaunted, but he is full of enthusiasm for the challenges that lie ahead. Having been the executive vice-president of Sony Music and president of his own Daylight label, Massey has developed superstar acts of every kind, including Anastacia, Good Charlotte, Shakira, and Oasis. Here he shares some of the insight gained in shaping those careers and reiterates the unchanging need for that musical catalyst that sparks the whole star-making process:

DAVID MASSEY: No matter what, you're going to need a phenomenal song. I'm not saying it should be a generic Top 40 radio song. I'm saying you need a statement, a real tailor-made defining statement, if you're going to build a star. A classic example would be Mariah Carey's "Vision of Love." Ideally, you need a huge melody and a lyric that's a great vehicle for what that artist is trying to subliminally say about him or herself.

In my experience, if you got the song off the shelf from a music publisher, already written, it's almost certainly not the right one. I've never had a hit that was given to me by a publisher. So much of what you receive is just generic. Therefore, it could be sung by anyone, and it doesn't define. Any hit I've ever had, if it didn't come directly from the artist, I've had to orchestrate the creation of it through enlisting great songwriters to write specifically for the project, often in collaboration with the artists themselves.

On Anastacia

When we first started with Anastacia, she wanted to do something in a funky, Sly and the Family Stone style. I knew it would be very hard to find a single in that vein that stood up. I was running Epic Records at the time, and Color Me Badd was signed to the label—Sam Watters, who was part of that group, would stop by my office occasionally. So one day, I told him about my problem with Anastacia. I said, "I want a great song for a big voice, kind of 'I Will Survive' but with a little more substance." Within three or four days, he came back and said, "I think I've got it." He played me the demo to "I'm Outta Love," in its earliest form.

That was the defining moment for Anastacia, once she had completed the song, performed it, and made it her own. Everything came from that great pairing of song and artist, and it led to a career that might never have exploded in that way. When you can put the subliminal personality of the artist into the song in a way that fits, it creates magnetism to which the public then reacts.

I'm also very conscious of what I call the "gag." The gag with "I'm Outta Love" was that everyone who heard that song imagined a big, older soul singer. Instead, what popped out was this young, blonde girl from Chicago with that massive voice. That was a great surprise and a great identity for her. I think it's why we sold 5 million records on her debut album.

A few years later, on "Left Outside Alone," which was the first single of her third album, we tried something else. Anastacia sang the opening to that song operatically, so it was almost impossible for anyone to recognize the voice. There were people within the company who were horrified at the idea of not spelling it out that it was Anastacia. But both she and I really wanted to do that, because it was the gag. It broke all the rules—and it worked brilliantly.

Every time I've taken a risk, I've been happy. Every time I've taken a sensible risk that was musically good, it pretty well always worked. On top of that, it's always been hugely satisfying.

On Oasis

"Wonderwall" was one of the most reactive songs I've ever been involved with. The album jumped more than a hundred places on the *Billboard* charts in just a few weeks, based on airplay on that one song. It was a hit in every part of the world. That's the power of a reactive song. Although it was a very unconventional lyric, a love song actually, it defined what Oasis was so good at. It showed that area beyond being just a rock 'n' roll band.

On Good Charlotte

Good Charlotte came into my office and said they had an idea for a song called "Lifestyles of the Rich and Famous." The line they had was "Lifestyles of the rich and famous/And you're always complaining." As soon as I heard it, I promised them if they could get that song done, it would be their breakthrough hit. It was a phenomenal idea, even in its rudimentary form. It absolutely did define them.

On Today's Music Business

I can't believe in this new world, how thirsty the public is for really fun, fresh, intelligent ideas. I've never seen this before. With Duffy, we've had great success, because we took some chances. Those risks are worth it. It isn't about the conventional way of selling CDs anymore. There is so much access to music, in a far more democratic way, that the more you can make a statement that's original, the more impact you'll make. But you must have those singles that separate and define. That's the hardest thing to find.

No matter what the business model is, whether it's going to be played on the radio or distributed online, we still end up with the hit. You still need the magical connection between the public and this particular piece of music. Ultimately, that's what it's all about.

Tuning into the Big Picture

For most songwriters, one of the job's most challenging aspects is the isolating nature of the work itself. Long hours locked in the studio searching for the right rhyme or the perfect chord change can lead to a dangerous case of tunnel vision. Great songs may be conceived in splendid solitude, but that's not how hits are made.

The process by which songs become hits is a collaborative one, and to contribute to it, you need a viewpoint that sees more than the simple nuts and bolts of songwriting. Only when you understand A&R's need for a single can you give the record label the kind of song they need. Once you're familiar with the kind of relentless research your song will face at radio, you'll make sure that you have a hook strong enough to pass the test. To see your song as the spark plug to the star-making machine is to know that something "catchy" is not enough. Your song has to define an identity for the artist that sings it.

To write a hit song, you need to know about more than songwriting.

Hit songwriters learn to think like A&R people, radio programmers, and music marketers. Then they use that knowledge in every stage of a song's development.

Your challenge will be to maintain this new, widescreen perspective, even as we narrow our focus to more specific songwriting techniques. In Part Two, you'll discover strategies to help meet the different and sometimes conflicting needs of all the players involved in turning a song into a hit. Now that you know how the game is played, all you need is a plan.

Part Two
The Hit Formula

CHAPTER FIVE

The Recipe for a Hit

Expect the Unexpected

Have you ever seen one of those movies in which nothing seems to make any sense? None of the plot ties together; you can't be quite sure if it's a drama or a comedy; things keep happening, but the events are all rather pointless? Pretty frustrating, huh? It's a good thing someone invented popcorn.

Or what about those movies where you just know what's going to happen from the first frame? Every turn in the plot is predictable; every character is obvious; every punch line is telegraphed long before it's delivered. It doesn't exactly keep you on the edge of your seat.

The truth illuminated here goes all the way back to the beginnings of storytelling, music, and drama. It is as old as Aristotle's *Poetics*. It is as fundamental as the blues, which is all about tension and release—three lines of repetition and a twist in the fourth and final line. It is also as modern as any song in today's Top 40. One basic principle that underlies all dramatic structure is that any work of art requires a proper balance between the comfort of the predictable and the surprise of the unexpected. If there is too much that is unpredictable, the audience will find only chaos. If the audience always gets what they expect, they will be bored.

Comfort and surprise. Tension and release. Three lines repeated and then something new. This is the rhythm of art.

If you purchased this book hoping to find one simple formula for creating hit songs, you're probably wondering just how far you'll have to read before it shows up. The truth is, you've already read it. That hallowed secret was actually revealed back in chapter two. Nevertheless, it warrants repeating. It comes from Hosh Gureli, the former radio MD and current A&R consultant. If you truly want to know what makes a hit, then look to Hosh for the answer:

A hit song has something special–it's different, but not too different. That's the formula the best writers know how to use.

A hit is different, but not too different. Granted, it's not the wisdom of Aristotle. Still, it is a pretty apt summary of the principle that underlies all commercial songwriting. When record labels insist on finding a song that's "edgy," it's just another way of saying that they need something "different." Radio's demand for songs that fit the format and blend with the rotation means that a song shouldn't be "too different." The challenge lies in striking the balance.

Too many songwriters put all their effort into one side of the equation or the other. The more commercially minded types, the craftsmen, concentrate entirely on creating music that echoes whatever is popular at the moment. "Doesn't it sound exactly like what's on the radio?" they exclaim. Indeed it does—and it's boring. There's nothing different about it.

Other more "artistic" types pride themselves on continually breaking new ground in every aspect of their songwriting. Any idea that doesn't feel entirely "original" is immediately dismissed as "derivative" or "typical." "You've never heard anything like this before," the writer promises. Most of the time, we will not wish to hear anything like it again. It's not a hit. It's too different.

To make this formula work effectively, each element in the equation must be valued appropriately. There can be no release without the tension. There's no surprise without the familiar. So let's begin by breaking the formula into its key components, to be sure that each receives its due.

The Comfort of the Familiar

It doesn't sound very exciting, does it? It's not exactly the stuff of which Grammy awards are made. Yet if we examine our own lives, we probably value our routines, habits, favorite places, and friends much more than we enjoy venturing forth into unknown territory or rooms filled with strangers. Few of us would choose a life of constant adventure or challenge. Most people prefer a generally comfortable existence, with the occasional shot of excitement.

We shouldn't be embarrassed by this. The familiar allows us to feel comfortable, confident, and in control of our lives. In fact, familiarity gives us the security to occasionally venture out and experience something new and different. Simply judging by the enduring presence of social constructs like home, family, property, and daily routine across almost every culture throughout history, one would conclude that this is just the way the human animal is wired. We need structure, predictability, and repetition.

What does this have to do with music? Plenty. Most of us don't enjoy chaos in our music any more than we enjoy it in our lives. Much of popular music's appeal lies in its predictability—the regularity of four, eight, and twelve measure sections; the restrictions of key and tonality that make things sound "in tune"; and the logic of a chord sequence that goes from a resting point, to a point of tension, and then returns to a resting point once again. This basic foundation is something we can easily understand, and it allows us to relax into the experience of listening.

Each time we hear a new song, we bring a subconscious set of expectations, based on all the music we've heard in the past. Of course, we don't expect that everything will be the same as before. That would be boring. We do expect that some of the basic structures and patterns that we've listened to in similar music will also be present in the new piece. Just like food in the fridge and a soft pillow makes one feel at home, there are certain fundamental qualities within songs of every genre that provide the listener with the comfort of the familiar: structure, repetition, simplicity, and a common language.

Structure: The Blueprint in Our Mind

I once went to visit someone who had designed his own home without any help from an architect. While the house itself was attractive, I immediately found it was impossible to find my way from room to room. I'd never realized how many assumptions one brings to the floor plan of a home. When these expectations are violated, a visitor in even a moderately sized house wanders around as if lost in Windsor Castle.

Songs have their own architecture as well, and the various song forms are deeply ingrained in the minds of the listening audience, whether they know it or not. While popular song structures do vary from period to period and genre to genre, even casual music listeners are intuitively familiar with the most common ways of organizing a musical composition.

Today, most songs use a repeating verse/pre-chorus/chorus structure (A-B-C), which is sometimes followed by a bridge section (A-B-C-D), and a final return to the chorus. While there may be additional instrumental sections, or slight abbreviations of sections when they repeat, it's rarely difficult to follow the form of a modern popular song. It's part of every music fan's built-in, pop-cultural awareness.

People with no technical knowledge of music can feel what's supposed to happen in a standard song form. Even a casual listener can intuit that after an eight-bar introduction, an eight-bar verse, and an eight-bar pre-chorus, it's time to get to the chorus. In fact, if the song doesn't go to the chorus at that point, the listener will be disappointed. Unease sets in. Silently, he or she wonders, "Did I miss it? Did we already have the chorus? Is there no chorus?

Is there any point to this song? How much longer will this hook-free song go on?"

Knowing where we are and where we are going is an essential part of our comfort zone. If a listener is lost, he or she will conclude that the song doesn't make sense and quit paying attention. Within seconds, the listener is doing the aural equivalent of wandering down a back stairwell in that sprawling self-designed house, looking for the nearest way out.

Repetition: Do It till You're Satisfied

Repetition is boring, predictable, and unoriginal, right? Certainly, it can be. On the other hand, few of us complain about the repetition of eating every day or receiving a weekly paycheck. Here's an alternate view of repetition:

Repetition is reliable. It's memorable. At least as it pertains to popular music, there is no rhythm, melody, or structure without repetition.

It's not an accident that any form of dance music, from polka to house to hip-hop, is based on rhythmic repetition. People looking to dance demand a steady, predictable rhythmic pattern. As any club DJ or society big band could tell you, repetition is essential to creating a groove; the groove is what inspires an audience to move. If you thought it was unnerving asking someone to dance, imagine if the band were changing tempos in every measure of the song. I think we'd all sit that one out.

Repetition is just as important in regard to melodies as it is to rhythm. Imagine trying to sing along to a melody that was entirely unpredictable. Any effective eight-bar melodic idea will consist of a melodic theme, some repetition of that theme, a few variations of the theme, and one or two surprises. Anyone listening to the car radio can intuitively recognize the pattern and anticipate where the melody will go. By the third time the chorus rolls around, driver and passengers are singing along. It's the repetition of melodic phrases, and the predictability of the theme-and-variation pattern, that makes the tune memorable.

In *Improvising Jazz* (New York: Fireside, 1987), Jerry Coker's seminal book on jazz improvisation (which is essentially the art of creating effective melodies on the spot), the author describes the unconscious game going on all the time between a listener and the melody maker, whether he or she is a jazz improviser or a song-writer. A listener can't help but predict whether the next musical phrase will be the same as the one that came before or something different. If everything in the song is repetitive, the game is too easy and the listener will lose interest. Conversely, if nothing ever repeats, the game will be impossible, and the listener will grow frustrated and tune out. Coker quotes Richmond Browne, a jazz pianist and instructor of theory at Yale University, who breaks it down bluntly: "Too much difference is sameness: boring. Too much sameness is boring—but also different once in a while."

It sounds a lot like Hosh Gureli's formula of "different, but not too different." Sometimes, all it takes is a slight variation in phrasing or inflection to keep a repetitive melody from growing predictable. As any good extended dance mix will prove, extreme repetition can also be interesting, as it heightens the tension and expectation for the inevitable release. So long as you avoid driving a listener to distraction or deadening the dynamics of the song, it's fair to say that the more repetitious a melody is, the more memorable it will be.

Simplicity: Sing a Simple Song

Martin Scorsese once said, "There's no such thing as simple. Simple is hard." Almost any artist in any medium will share the sentiment. Simplicity requires a constant paring down, editing, and narrowing of focus until only the essential elements remain. To make something look or feel simple can be very difficult and painful for the creator.

Yet, it makes things very easy for the audience—and that's the point. By stripping away everything that is superfluous, a songwriter makes an immediate impact and removes an audience's natural doubt and impatience ("I'll bet I'm not going to like this."). By clearing away unnecessary ornamentation, the songwriter lessens the risk of any confusion or distractions ("I can't follow all this."). Simplicity builds trust. It encourages an audience to let down their guard and be drawn in from the heart, rather than the head.

No matter how interesting they may be, unnecessary elements in a song will only distract the listener. Lyrics that are too wordy will make it impossible to feel the emotion. Melodies that are too busy will pull the listener out of the rhythmic groove. Harmonic progressions full of dense, complex chords will detract from the melody. By trying to do too much with any one component of the song, you can bring the entire enterprise crashing down.

On the other hand, when a song is simple, all the elements work together with a common goal: to make sure that the listener "gets" what the song is trying to say. This unity of purpose gives a simple song an emotional power that often remains beyond the reach of more sophisticated compositions. As brilliant and intricate as his early lyrics like "Jungleland" were, Bruce Springsteen reached a far larger audience with simpler songs like "Dancing in the Dark." In commercial terms, simplicity is the difference between being the critic's choice and being a superstar.

A Common Language: Ya Know What I'm Talkin' About?

If you've ever been lost in a foreign country, you know what a relief it can be to find someone who speaks your language. Suddenly you can relax, get your bearings, and begin to feel more comfortable in a new environment.

While it's often said that music is the universal language, the truth is that music speaks in a thousand different tongues, many of them almost indecipherable to an outsider. A hip-hop lyric might as well come with subtitles for all the sense it would make to an opera fan. A line about "an old plywood boat with a '75 Johnson with electric choke" in an Alan Jackson song would be lost on a techno club audience.

It goes beyond lyrics. Because of its similarity to the Irish classic "Danny Boy," a melody like "You Raise Me Up," has immediate resonance with a classical crossover audience—but probably not with a contemporary urban one. On the other hand, hip-hop and dance records are filled with obscure samples that are nevertheless instantly recognizable to the crowd in the clubs.

All such elements—the attention to descriptive detail or the use of slang in a lyric, a familiar sample or keyboard sound, a melody or chord progression that recalls another song or time period—send a message from the songwriter to the listener:

Relax. We speak the same language.

A common language conveys a deeper bond of shared history and values. It proves the song and the singer's authenticity and makes both the artist and the listener part of something larger than themselves. When Gretchen Wilson sang about "redneck girls like me," she was inviting everyone who listened and understood to join her circle of friends. When Busta Rhymes calls out "Pass the Courvoisier," he's extending the same invitation to a very different audience.

That bond is the ultimate reward for basing your work in the familiar. Most of us are drawn to people with whom we have something in common. Through the use of structure, repetition, simplicity, and a common language, a songwriter creates a comfort zone of trust and security with the listener. Once that foundation of trust and security is established, a listener is ready for a little jolt of something new.

The Shock of Surprise

First of all, let it be said: Nothing is all that new. After all, there are several thousand years of musical history behind us. Even when we think we've created a unique song, we can rest assured that another writer probably came up with a similar sound or lyric at some point in history. None of us should expect to devise a new, earth-shattering innovation each time we sit down to write.

But we should seek to surprise. A surprise is less a matter of invention than juxtaposition. When we surprise, we place the familiar in a new context. For instance: We may be very familiar with the people in our office. Nevertheless, if all of them suddenly show up in a restaurant where we think we're meeting our uncle for a quiet birthday lunch, then we are surprised. It's not that our office mates are suddenly shocking. We're surprised to see them in an unexpected context. In the day-to-day world of songwriting, this kind of surprise element, "the fish out of water," is what's used most often to make a song sound different.

The Visitor from Another Planet

Think of it as the "Mork and Mindy" effect. For those too young to remember, *Mork and Mindy* was the popular sitcom in which Robin Williams first became a star. He played the role of Mork, an alien being from the planet Ork, who was living with Mindy, an average single girl in Boulder, Colorado. The humor of the show came from watching the mundane adventures of daily life, thrown a little off-kilter by the presence of a guy from outer space.

The same trick will work for putting a little surprise in your song. By suddenly introducing one musical element from "outer space," something not expected within a particular musical genre, you create a sound that feels new and fresh. When Blondie created "Rapture," it wasn't that they invented rap. They simply put it in the context of a pop-rock song, and it sounded new to the audience that heard it. When Run-DMC released "King of Rock," it wasn't the first time that anyone had heard rock guitar riffs. It was the first time that anyone had heard them in a rap song, and that was enough to provide the surprise.

It's very important to notice the difference between using a musical element borrowed from another style to add interest and novelty and actually trying to combine two styles, which, as we've said, often leads to a long fall through the cracks. Run-DMC was very clearly making a rap record, to which they added a few rock elements. In the same way, Linkin Park uses a few rap elements in what are distinctly rock records, aimed at a rock audience. But neither Run-DMC nor Linkin Park is a rap-rock act.

The introduction of different elements into unexpected contexts keeps popular music vibrant. Whether it's The Beatles introducing harmonic and orchestral influences from the classical world, The Police borrowing world-beat rhythms, or Cee-Lo putting sixties-style soul melodies over European-sounding club tracks, almost all of popular music history can be traced through the intermingling of ideas from different musical worlds. Rock 'n' roll was created when rhythm and blues met country. Disco was created when Philly soul met European electronic dance music.

For the professional songwriter, this mixing of influences is an everyday reality. A&R people may ask for a song that sounds just like the number-one record that week. Experienced songwriters know better. The A&R person needs something "different, but not too different." This means constructing something similar to the hit of the week but adding an unexpected element—a rhythmic approach, an instrumental sound, a lyrical attitude, a melodic pattern—from an older style, a different genre, or another song. Fire meets gasoline; East meets West; Mork meets Mindy, and... surprise!

Successful songwriters usually opt for small surprises, rather than grand innovations. Even the most experimental writer could only hope to come up with one or two brand new ideas within a career. In most cases, all that a song needs to set it apart is one or two moments that defy the listener's expectation. Just as a joke requires a punch line, and a plotline requires an unexpected turn, every song needs a twist.

Do the Twist

While the prospect of inventing entirely new musical ideas on a daily basis is beyond almost every writer, the challenge of adding a twist or two to every song is entirely plausible. You can accomplish this by anticipating what a listener expects (the familiar) and giving him or her something else instead—hopefully something better, more emotionally satisfying, more interesting. As a songwriter, your job is to provide a twist. Your success will be determined by how creative your twist is. A good twist yields a good song; a great twist makes a hit.

THE TURN OF THE PHRASE Nothing makes for a more effective twist than a clever lyrical turn of phrase. In most cases, this means taking a familiar word or catchphrase and giving it a new or unexpected meaning. We all know about milkshakes, but Kelis gave it a new twist in "Milkshake." Fergie did the same thing with "London Bridge." These are instances of using a word or phrase as a metaphor. Country writers like to play on double mean-ings with titles like "If I Said You Had a Beautiful Body Would You Hold It Against Me." Sometimes, you can even invent a new word—like Destiny's Child's "Bug A Boo" or Trace Adkins's "Honky Tonk Badonkadonk."

The Songwriter's Challenge

While you're looking through a magazine or a newspaper or watching television, try jotting down five words or phrases that catch your attention. Then take that list and try to twist each word or phrase into the title of a song. Could the word be a metaphor for something else? Could the phrase have a double meaning? Can you use the word as a basis for an entirely new phrase?

Country songwriting legend Mac Davis once had a television variety show, where one of the most popular features involved the audience tossing out song titles and Mac writing a chorus to that title on the spot. It's a great exercise in learning to put a turn on a phrase.

CHANGING THE TUNE Any effective melody can be analyzed as a motif or theme (the basic three- or four-note melodic shape), some variations on that theme (the repetition), and an unexpected melodic leap or dip leading into a new melodic shape (the change of tune). We'll talk more about the nuances of melodic construction in chapter eight. But here's a basic rule with a good pedigree:

Mozart maintained that a melodic motif could be repeated once, but the third phrase would have to represent a change. In other words: phrase, repeat of phrase, then variation.

It's a natural rhythm of familiarity and surprise that still feels right today. Think back to a melody like "What a Fool Believes."* Notice how the melody introduces a basic melodic idea:

"But what a fool believes..."

That's followed by another repetition of the same melody, with a slight variation:

"He sees..."

And then a concluding phrase, that's both a surprise and a variation on the opening melody of the verse:

"Is always better than nothing."

---

* "What a Fool Believes," words and music by Kenny Loggins and Michael McDonald. © 1978, 1979, Snug Music and Milk Money Music. All rights for Snug Music administered by Wixen Music Publishing, Inc. All rights reserved. Used by permission of Alfred Publishing Company, Inc. and Wixen Music Publishing, Inc.

The Songwriter's Challenge

Start by singing a simple melodic phrase—it could be anywhere from three to six notes. It doesn't even have to be original; perhaps it's something you've heard before. Repeat it. Then repeat it once again, but alter it just slightly—try starting the phrase a half a beat later or adding just one or two more notes. Let this variation lead you into the "change of tune"—a leap up to a new note, or a switch in the melodic direction, or a change of the melodic rhythm—that will finish off the musical phrase.

Your original melodic phrase does not have to be wildly inventive. It's the "change" in the final phrase that makes the magic. As a songwriter, the challenge is to develop an intuitive sense of when a phrase needs to be repeated or echoed and when it's time to change the game for the listener, by introducing a melodic surprise.

SAYING THE UNSPEAKABLE Have you ever thought about how many hit songs—from "Who Let the Dogs Out?" to

"I Believe I Can Fly"—are not about romantic love? I'm always amazed at the number of writers who focus almost exclusively on love and romance as lyrical subject matter, despite the vast and diverse terrain explored in the past.

The rest of the listening audience has noticed this as well. When we hear a song for the first time, the unspoken assumption is that it will have a romantic storyline. By turning instead to an unexpected subject, especially a controversial or provocative one, the writer can instantly add a twist that will make the song stand out. Songs about child abuse ("Luka"), poverty ("Inner City Blues [Make Me Wanna Holler]"), abortion ("Papa Don't Preach"), or politics ("Sunday Bloody Sunday") show that pop music can effectively address almost any social issue. Songs about baseball ("Centerfield"), cars ("Little Deuce Coupe"), and fashion ("Chain Hang Low") work as well. Any subject is a welcome relief from the expectation of another breakup or make-up song.

The Songwriter's Challenge

Take a finished lyric, or one of the five phrases you wrote down for the "turn of phrase" exercise on page 109. Leaving the title or catchphrase as is, can you put a twist on it by constructing a chorus idea that isn't a straightforward love song? Look at what Sara Bareilles did with "Love Song," as she flips a potentially romantic lyric into a refusal to write a love song. Think about other topics that concern you, whether it's politics or partying. Nothing is off limits.

Dare to Be Different... But Not Too Different

The greatest challenge in balancing the comfort of the familiar and the shock of surprise lies in conquering that arch enemy of creators everywhere: fear. The songwriter who avoids the twist and opts for writing something "not too different" is surrendering to the fear that an unexpected lyric line or an unconventional chord might turn a listener off. In the same way, a writer who insists on avoiding anything predictable or typical is also giving in to fear—the fear of being deemed "unoriginal."

A confident writer knows the value of the familiar and isn't afraid to study what other writers are doing or to learn from what's worked in the past. If you know that you have a solid twist where it counts, then you can let the song settle into a structure and language that the listener will understand easily.

At the same time, you can't create a twist unless you're willing to take a risk on the unexpected. Just as a comedian has no assurance that a punch line will draw a laugh, a songwriter never knows if a twist will sound weird and wonderful or just plain weird.

It takes courage to be different and honesty to know when you're trying to be too different. But without the twist, there's nothing to make the song stand out.

For better or worse, songwriting is a "winner takes all" proposition. There are no consolation prizes for those who play it too safe and predictable. Just as David Massey mentioned in chapter four, the rewards come to those who trust their own instincts and gamble on an original idea.

CHAPTER SIX

The Flavor of a Hit
Fresh and Long Lasting

Suddenly, everyone wants to be a music publisher. After years of living in the shadow of the larger and more glamorous record industry, music publishing is the place to be these days. Even as media pundits predict the imminent demise of the music business, new publishing companies seem to sprout up almost weekly, seeking to acquire catalogs of songs for sums that can stretch into the millions of dollars.

As a music publisher myself, I'm not surprised that many view this particular segment of the music business as a safe port during a raging storm. Unlike a record company, which owns and controls a physical product—that is, the actual sound recording of a song—music publishers own or control the song itself. Aside from occasionally printing sheet music, a music publisher doesn't manufacture a product. Instead, the music publisher makes money by issuing licenses. The publisher of a song grants licenses to record labels, movie studios, television stations, advertisers, and others, allowing them (for a price) to use that particular song on a record, in a movie, on television, in an advertisement, or wherever else one might find music in the course of daily life. In an age when few consumers are buying CDs, but people are listening to more music than ever before, this licensing role is a very good business indeed.

The investment industry bean counters have figured this out. Today, new music publishing companies are not the work of wide-eyed entrepreneurs with big artistic dreams. Rather, they are ventures put together by conservative number-crunchers from the gray-suited world of banking and high finance. As a long-term investment strategy, hedge funds, banks, and money managers seek to acquire catalogs of past and present hit songs. Suddenly it seems, the financial world has come to a realization:

Hit songs have value.

Any Cadillac salesman working near Nashville's Music Row could have vouched for that. What's now apparent is that hit songs tend to maintain their value over long periods of time. Classic hits are covered by new artists, played on oldies stations, sampled on hip-hop records, and put in advertisements. As a result, year after year, they just keep earning money. Today, investors discuss hit songs in the same breath as Old Master paintings, real estate, and gold bullion. In most cases, no one could be more surprised than the songwriters themselves.

It's almost impossible to write a timeless, universal song by setting out with that goal in mind. The pressure of an impending release date or the potential to cash in on a new dance craze fueled the creation of most classics. Few enduring songs started from the hope of leaving a lasting imprint on popular culture. To music publishers, songs are a long-term investment. For songwriters, they exist largely in the here and now.

As I said in chapter one, one of the chief characteristics of a "single" is that it must be timely. Unlike a painting, which could hang on a wall in obscurity for decades, only to be rediscovered by an art critic and deemed a masterpiece, a song has to work immediately for the target audience to have any future chance at timelessness or universal appeal. Seldom is a flop single later resurrected and turned into a classic. Hit songs may hold their value, but they have to become hits first. Consequently, most songwriters don't have the luxury of worrying much about posterity.

And yet, who wouldn't want to write something with staying power? As our friends from Wall Street would point out, longevity is where the real money lies. When it comes to creating classic songs, we need a formula that will work for today, but also for tomorrow. It's not enough to say that a hit is made up of the "comfort of the familiar and the shock of surprise." Like a good piece of chewing gum, a hit must also be "fresh and long lasting."

Just as there is an inherent tension in the formula of "different, but not too different," there is a natural push and pull between a song's need to appeal to today's audience and yet also stand the test of time. Songwriters perform a balancing act, trying to keep the song fresh, but never forgetting that "long lasting" is the ultimate goal. The only way to accomplish this is by acknowledging that music functions on three different levels: It is fashion, it is cultural expression, and ultimately, it's an art form that endures.

Music as Fashion

Fashion is funny. If you've ever looked through a fashion magazine, there's something comical about the seasonal dictates that supposedly reflect the public's changing tastes but that feel more as if they've been imposed by royal decree. This season, skirts are short, pants are thin, and green is the new black. Says who? No one knows.

But for devoted fashionistas, the motive that drives this constant change is anything but frivolous. Fashion, to be fashionable, must always be fresh. It must capture the present tense in a unique way, reflecting how people live and look and behave today. Tomorrow everything changes. In other words, it's a lot like popular music.

You can't criticize fashion for being trendy. It would be like criticizing water for being wet. Trendiness is the nature of fashion. Likewise, people who lament the trendiness of the Top 40 are missing a large part of its appeal. Popular music is fun because it is a constant work in progress, capturing all the energy, emotion, brilliance, and silliness of its time. Some of it wears well, and plenty of it sounds ridiculous just a few years later. That's why it's entertaining.

It's also why a technical knowledge of music alone cannot make someone a hit songwriter, any more than knowledge of tailoring can turn someone into a successful fashion designer. Those who create fashion or music need a sense of style—that mysterious radar that captures the mood of the times. They need to understand intuitively what's new and what's passé and what is about to become cool in a month or two.

In musical terms, a sense of style means knowing what musical fashions are in and out of favor and which might be ready to make a return. It requires you to understand what rhythms people are moving to, what instruments sound contemporary, or what effects, samples, or gimmicks sound fresh and which ones have been used once too often. It demands a keen sense of what lyrical subjects, phrases, or slang are relevant.

That kind of musical fashion sense has been characteristic of important songwriters from Cole Porter to Bono to Prince. Look at the lyric to "You're the Top," or the music of U2's "Pop," or the blend of sixties psychedelia and James Brown funk influences that shaped the *Purple Rain* album. The Beatles showed a perfect ear for popular culture as they moved from the simple, brash sound of the British Invasion to more sophisticated, conceptual pieces like *Sgt. Pepper's*. The Rolling Stones even captured the disco era with "Miss You." Billy Joel went from "Piano Man" to catching the spirit of New Wave with "It's Still Rock & Roll to Me." A sense of style simply means a restless desire for change and a constant effort to better capture the spirit of the times. Ralph Gleason, in writing of jazz legend Miles Davis, said, "The greatest single thing about Miles Davis is that, like Picasso and Duke Ellington and Bob Dylan, he does not stand still." That's fashion—and it's pretty good company to keep.

When it comes to understanding music as fashion, the songwriter's challenge is to look forward and backward simultaneously.

It's not enough to anticipate the latest trends and copy them. You also have to understand what the trends represent and how they relate to what's come before. This means anticipating the future trends, in the context of the past.

Because they both focus relentlessly on the "new," fashion and popular music are often decidedly youth oriented. Cutting-edge trends in these areas of culture typically emerge from teenagers, or twenty-somethings, as they struggle to create their own and their generation's identity. Particularly for songwriters working in the pop or urban market, it's important to remain "young" in your sensibility and to keep an eye on what's happening in junior high schools, high schools, and colleges. Most often, this is where the trends are set.

At the same time, a pop songwriter has to keep the other eye on the past. As I discussed in chapter four, no one can create genuinely new art all the time. Fashion constantly plunders its own history, reviving the miniskirt, or the military look, or (yikes) those MC Hammer balloon pants. In the same way, music constantly grabs sounds, styles, and attitudes from other generations and updates them for a new era. Nothing ever quite comes back exactly the way it was, but almost every style or sound gets revived eventually.

Always in Vogue and into the Groove: Madonna

When it comes to working the runway of musical fashions, no one strikes a pose, or poses, like Madonna. Much has been made of

Madonna's unfailing instincts for remaking her visual image album by album, throughout her long and varied career. Equal attention should be paid to her ability to re-create and update her musical sound persistently.

If you compare her eighties dance classics like "Into the Groove" (with its freestyle and Hi-NRG influences) to mainstream pop records like "Papa Don't Preach" (underpinned with influences from the fifties and sixties) to the progressive, electronica vibe of "Ray of Light," or the *Hard Candy* collaborations with urban producers like Timbaland and Nate "Danja" Hills, you can see a songwriter determined to remain contemporary and to deliver hit songs that are perfectly in step with the times.

So how does she do it? Here are four fashion tips you can pick up from a little Madonna-watching:

KEEP AN EAR TO THE STREET Stories abound of Madonna turning up unexpectedly in after-hours New York nightclubs: in the booth with cutting-edge DJs like Junior Vasquez, watching the dancers, trying out new music, and checking out the hottest records of the moment.

TRAVEL WITH THE "IN" CROWD Much of our taste is defined by the company we keep. From eighties DJ Jellybean Benitez, to polished pop producers like Pat Leonard, to collaborations with Lenny Kravitz, to her new association with Justin Timberlake, Madonna has created an ever-evolving supporting cast of collaborators that move her in new directions and challenge her to remain on the cutting edge.

KEEP AN EYE OUTSIDE THE MUSIC BUSINESS The world is bigger than the recording studio and the record company office. Like the East Village club scene that spawned her, Madonna is equal parts fashion, music, dance, theater, film, and art. Her circle is big enough to encompass Donatella Versace and Andrew Lloyd Webber, Guy Ritchie and Willi Ninja. In this era, every art form intersects with the other. Madonna manages always to be at the intersection.

GO WITH THE FLOW—ADAPT Some people say change is good. Change is just change. Adapting is good. Don't believe it? Ask a dinosaur, if you can find one. There is no escaping the fact that life always mutates. The artists that forge long and varied careers don't waste energy fighting change, or bemoaning it. They are fascinated and energized by it. Madonna knows that the first law of survival is to adapt.

Music as Cultural Expression

The downside of equating music with fashion is that it makes it all seem a bit frivolous. Obviously, a song that feels fresh will be more entertaining than a song that feels dated or passé, yet there's more at stake than just entertainment value. A hit not only needs to be fashionable; it needs to be relevant.

While most fashion is concerned primarily with appearances, music seeks to be a means of cultural expression, which means it delivers messages about human relationships, social issues, politics, and identity. Part of the job of the songwriter is to capture and interpret the way we live today and to provide a unique perspective on what's happening in the world. In that respect, creating a song that feels fresh means saying something that is relevant to your audience today.

In 1972, "I Am Woman" was a very militant expression of the desire for female empowerment. It perfectly captured that particular moment in time. Today, Pink's "Stupid Girls" conveys a similar idea but from the perspective of a different generation. There will always be room for a new song or a new songwriter, simply because the times are always changing.

Of course, to embrace music as cultural expression forces us to acknowledge that the pool of potential subjects for songs is much deeper than "me, myself, and I." We've already suggested that there may be more interesting things to write about than romantic relationships, particularly ones that are very personal. So why not try writing about something broader, or more reflective of our society as a whole? If you pick a subject that directly relates to contemporary life, your song will feel fresh, relevant, and timely.

Even if you still insist on writing about your boyfriend or girlfriend, you could at least try to see the relationship from a larger perspective. If social issues like racial tension, economic inequality, or changing gender roles affect our lives and relationships, then they should also affect our love songs. Think of how a song like John Mayer's "Daughters" uses a romantic relationship as the springboard to addressing the impact that a dysfunctional family can have on a child. In today's world, love is not always simple. Our love songs should capture that complexity.

The idea of music as cultural expression isn't only a matter of lyrics. As society evolves, musicians, composers, and producers also try to reflect those changes on a musical level. It wasn't coincidence that the folk revival of the sixties coincided with the peace movement and the civil rights struggles. The disco craze of the seventies was in many ways a musical expression of the sexual revolution. Today, the craze for mash-ups, in which underground DJs or producers combine two separate and often completely unrelated records into one new track, is a perfect reflection of our information age, the influence of technology, and the anti-"star" ethos that fuels reality TV.

Making Music That Matters: Don Henley

While many songwriters have managed to capture the cultural moment for at least a split second, far fewer succeed at it over and over, across several decades. Don Henley has chronicled the changes in American society from his start with the Eagles in the seventies, through his solo career in the eighties and nineties, and up until the present time, with an accuracy and insight that rivals any journalist. With the Eagles, he captured the laid-back spirit of the California dream and followed it to its dissolution in "Hotel California." He caught the aging of the baby boomers with "The Boys of Summer" and the rise of the media culture with "Dirty Laundry."

Henley remains relevant not simply by adapting to the times but also by identifying how the world around him has transformed and interpreting for us what these changes mean. Here are four suggestions, based on Henley's work, for how to tackle the big issues and twist them into big hits.

PAINT A PICTURE Images speak louder than messages. No matter how weighty the topic, you're still writing a song. No one is interested in a sociological treatise put to music. When it comes to conveying the big picture, the truth lies in the small details.

There's no better way to convey the transition from the 1970s to the 1980s in America than "out on the road today, I saw a Deadhead sticker on a Cadillac." Nothing could better capture the dangerously seductive quality of the California dream than that "dark desert highway," the "cool wind," and the "warm smell of colitas, rising up through the air." Many of Henley's songs feel almost like photo-journals, with lyrical snapshots that convey tremendous meaning. Images like "Tequila Sunrise" or "Dirty Laundry" tell the story by themselves.

TELL A STORY It goes beyond finding the perfect image. Many Henley songs are themselves a kind of extended metaphor, in which the characters and plot carry a deeper, larger meaning. This is called an *allegory*, and it can be a songwriter's powerful tool.

A song like "All She Wants to Do Is Dance" feels like a mini-movie, complete with primary and supporting characters, sets, and a plotline. Immediately, we're pulled into a world of "wild pistol-wavers who aren't afraid to die," selling drugs and weapons while the girls dance for money with the foreigners. But when the protagonist "barely makes it to the airport" and hears the people shout, "Don't come back here, Yankee," we know that there is a larger meaning to the story. While we're being entertained, we're being sent a message about the times in which we live.

When grappling with big subjects, you need to avoid being preachy. Messages sent directly are likely to be tuned out. The allegory allows you to tell a small, entertaining story, while making a big point.

WRITE WHAT YOU KNOW Any attempt at cultural expression demands authenticity. The California lifestyle portrayed by Don Henley is different than the one captured by Brian Wilson. Both of those visions are radically different from the California depicted by Tupac Shakur or Jane's Addiction. Not one of these artists or writers would even attempt to capture the other's world, as it would immediately ring false.

Like many great novelists or filmmakers, Henley has a narrow but infinitely rich terrain that he draws upon—a landscape full of very specific characters, locations, and scenarios that are largely derived from his own life experience. As a rock superstar in the seventies, he was undoubtedly familiar with "Life in the Fast Lane." "The End of the Innocence" described the fading of youthful idealism in the Reagan years at a time when Henley was reaching middle age. It's very difficult to capture a cultural moment from the outside looking in. Draw your material from the world in which you live.

STAY OPEN—GET INVOLVED If you're writing what you know, it stands to reason that the more you know, the better you'll write. The more active you are socially, politically, and intellectually, the more interesting your ideas about society are likely to be. It's worth noting that Don Henley was awarded the MusiCares Person of the Year award in 2007, reflecting his work in causes that range from saving Walden Woods and Caddo Lake to the creation of the Recording Artists Coalition. By most accounts, Henley is an intellectually restless, socially engaged, opinionated, often combative person—not too different from the music he creates.

Sometimes, the best thing you can do for your songwriting is to take a little break. After all, your writing can only be relevant if it relates to the world beyond the recording studio isolation booth. In the interest of keeping your mind and your music fresh, it's good to get out once in a while. In an interview with Robert Santelli for *Modern Drummer* magazine, Henley himself acknowledges the value of a change of scenery or a new life experience to renew and expand your creative powers: "Between each album I try to gain a new insight that I didn't have before and perhaps write a song about something that I've written about before, but from a fresh viewpoint."

Music That Endures

When it comes to defining what we want our songs to be, we know that "fresh" is a worthy goal. We also know that "long lasting" is even better. Those investment bankers forking up nine-figure checks to buy publishing catalogs aren't looking for hot new hits. They're hungry for "classic" copyrights—songs that have stood the test of time. To view music as fashion or cultural expression might help us keep our songs fresh, but if we want them to stick around for generations to come, we need something more. We need to identify what gives a song staying power.

The problem is that most of the qualities that make a song sound fresh today will make the song feel stale five years later. The hot beat, the trendy effect or sample, or the lyrical line that drops the latest slang will inevitably be out of fashion relatively soon. A song that perfectly captures a particular moment in society will not be as relevant when the times change.

Or will it? In fact, it's very hard to predict which songs will endure and which won't. Those "dated" slang phrases or musical gimmicks might be exactly what bring the song back as nostalgia. Whatever luck and timing was required to create a hit song in the first place will be equally vital in sustaining a song for future generations. The right placement in an advertisement, or an unexpected cover by a contemporary superstar, can make all the difference as to whether a song survives or disappears permanently from the public memory.

Many songwriters, particularly the ones with formal musical training, often believe that serious, musically sophisticated ballads are more "classic" than up-tempos, but history doesn't bear that out. For every "Greatest Love of All" or "And I Am Telling You I'm Not Going" there's a "Beer Barrel Polka" or "Red Red Wine." The qualities that make a song long lasting are different from those that make a song fresh, but they are not necessarily at odds with each other. When you're looking at the really big picture of hit songwriting, a number of key concerns matter in the long run.

Simplicity Stays Fresh

When a songwriter tells me that he or she avoids that "throwaway pop stuff" and prefers instead to write things that can be classics, I usually know to expect a series of maudlin, musically intricate, lyrically dense songs that scream, "Take me seriously!" It's not a very good approach to writing a hit song for today, and it's an even worse approach for writing a hit for tomorrow and the days after. The one thing that most classic songs have in common is simplicity.

For even the most innovative songwriters, it's often the simplest songs that endure. With his blend of classical and jazz idioms, George Gershwin may have been the most musically sophisticated composer in the history of American pop music. Yet, it's the spiritual-like lullaby "Summertime" and the sparse, almost trifling "'S Wonderful" that define Gershwin for most contemporary audiences.

Simple songs are timeless, because they are infinitely adaptable. They can be rearranged in any style, rerecorded by dozens of different artists, and thus be renewed and reinvigorated again and again. Simplicity leaves room for interpretation, both by new artists and new generations of listeners.

Melody Lingers On

We all know that songs are made of four primary elements: melody, harmony, rhythm, and (at least in the case of popular songs) lyrics. This does not mean that all of those elements are equal in importance. In the end, it's melody that really matters.

No one goes away humming a chord pattern. In fact, harmonic progressions often date a song's sound. When a song is remade, the arrangers may choose to alter the chords to make it feel more contemporary or more fitting for a particular genre. Likewise, rhythmic patterns (beats, if you like) come and go as fast as the latest dance craze. Even lyrics, with their slang, topical references, and timely subject matter, often age quickly. The jazz repertoire includes countless "standard" songs, for which every jazzman knows the tune but none could quote a line of the lyric.

Ultimately, melody is what survives. Again, it comes down to adaptability. A memorable melody can persevere through almost any change to its surroundings. It can be reharmonized, set to a different beat, or played by virtually any instrument. It can be translated into other languages, made into a parody, or even stripped of its lyric altogether.

Even the most casual listener will recognize a song as long as the melody is left relatively intact. No one worries much about the chords to "Happy Birthday." No one needs a drummer for it either. I've heard it done in French and Italian, and I didn't understand a word. But trust me, it will be sung at your birthday for many years to come, because everyone knows the tune.

Drama Doesn't Date

Classical drama is built on big, basic human emotions: joy, sorrow, jealousy, revenge, love, hate. These feelings are timeless because they are integral to our humanity. They are not subject to fashion, political correctness, or changes in local custom. *King Lear* works in any generation and in the most contemporary or ancient setting. Drama doesn't date.

Manners, attitudes, and values, on the other hand, can make no such claim. Ambiguity, cynicism, irony, sarcasm, self-awareness, and the like are modern (or maybe postmodern) sensibilities typical of our contemporary culture. These are what you might call "small emotions." They're more a matter of nurture than nature, which is to say that they are approaches we learn from the society around us, rather than large, fundamental human emotions that are ours from birth. As such, their staying power is limited, and their appeal is less than universal.

Most classic songs appeal to us on a very basic dramatic level. They make us laugh, cry, dance, or rise up in anger. They don't make us grin at their cleverness, infer their meaning, or examine their politics. A classic song is not only simple in its language or form, but it is also simple in its emotional appeal. It focuses on the big feelings, rather than the small ones. "Standing in the Shadows of Love" is not subtle, and there's no mixed emotion. It's sung as if the singer's life depends on it. The same is true of "I'm So Lonesome I Could Cry." Unless human nature undergoes some pretty drastic changes, these two songs will remain as relevant fifty years from now as they were when they were written.

Anytime Is Party Time

For most people, music fulfills a relatively basic function: It's supposed to be fun. You play music at a party to get people dancing, or at a club to entertain the audience, or on the big date to set the mood. In that context, it's not hard to understand why there are as many fun and frivolous classics as dark and serious ones. Who hasn't danced to "In the Mood" at a wedding reception or watched a bar band put the crowd in a frenzy with "Mustang Sally"? And there probably isn't a sports fan alive who doesn't know "Who Let the Dogs Out?"

These songs are classics precisely because of how well they fit into a party atmosphere. Just as it was in societies a thousand years ago, music is part of our celebrations, festivals, and group events. We use it to revel together. By becoming part of our shared experience, the songs that we all enjoy at weddings, parties, nightclubs, and sporting events make their way from one generation to the next. This is how a song like "Take Me Out to the Ballgame" transcends time and remains a fan favorite for centuries. In the same way, new classics are made when parents and children do the electric slide at a wedding or the YMCA dance at the stadium. Whether it's Sousa's "Stars and Stripes Forever" or Kool & the Gang's "Celebration," the songs that get the crowd up on their feet are almost guaranteed to last.

Design for Today, Build for Tomorrow

Singer-songwriter Jackson Browne has said, "A song is like an instrument in that it can lay around for years, and somebody can pick it up and play it again.... The best ones get better with age."*

---

* Paul Zollo, *Songwriters on Songwriting* (Cambridge, MA: Da Capo Press, 1991).

Several years ago, my wife and I had the opportunity to restore an old stone farmhouse in the hills of Italy. Dating back to the 1700s, the house was constructed almost exclusively from materials found in the vicinity—stones, terra cotta tiles, and roughly cut wood beams—by a farmer simply looking for a roof over his head and a stable for his livestock. By the time my wife and I found it, the house had been abandoned for nearly fifty years and was in severe disrepair. A wayward step could send you plummeting through the floor and into the room below.

And yet, the house remained—still standing, and in many ways, made more beautiful with the passage of time. The natural materials and the architectural simplicity that were products of historical necessity are now the stuff that spawns a thousand Tuscan photo books. Old houses like this one were designed for the time in which they were built, using the technology at hand, and meeting the needs of the people who lived and worked inside. Nevertheless, because they were made with high-quality materials and great care, the homes endure for the future—a future the original builders could never have foreseen.

Whether he or she crafts houses or songs, the creator has no choice but to create for the present—it's the only time he or she knows. The potential to last long after the creator is gone lies in the execution.

If we accept the idea that music exists not just for its own sake but to serve a purpose in society, then the paradox of creating something both fresh and long lasting begins to solve itself. Clearly, if a new song is going to entertain, inspire, or enlighten us in the present, it must be timely, reflecting the fashion of the moment and giving meaning to our contemporary culture. If the songwriter captures the present effectively, that song just might have a chance at enduring for generations.

CHAPTER SEVEN

The Framework of a Hit

Form and Substance

In case you haven't noticed, the hit-writing formulas established thus far, "different, but not too different" and "fresh, and long lasting," are less than precise. In fact, they feel like oxymorons, suggesting a first step, negated by a second step. As instructions go, they leave a lot of room for interpretation.

That's intentional. The magic of a hit song lies in the tension between two different impulses. There is the comfort of the familiar and the shock of surprise. There is the trendiness of music as fashion and the timelessness of music for the ages. As I mentioned at the outset, anyone seeking absolute rules will be disappointed. If you want to discover what makes a hit, be prepared for plenty of trial and error.

These formulas are frameworks on which a unique composition can be built. If you've ever tried cooking from a recipe, you know that following the basic instructions won't always yield a dish that looks like the picture in the book. Perfect adherence to the steps still won't make you a master chef. Culinary artists use a recipe as a framework on which they can improvise, experiment, and ultimately whip up a new dish. Any formula that leaves no room for interpretation will yield formulaic results. It will be all form and no substance.

When it comes to songwriting, the first part of the hit formula is the "form": a predictable, understandable structure; with a logical sequencing of verse, chorus, and bridge; and the effective use of repetition. Form ensures that your music is not "too different." The proper form means that your song will "fit the format" at radio.

Songs that get the form right sound like hits, even if they later prove not to be. Songs with the correct form are those that are selected as singles. They are the ones that radio agrees to put into testing. A songwriter who masters the form in the formula can carve out a good, if unremarkable, career in the music business. When it comes to genuine success, though, form by itself is not enough.

A hit needs a little bit of substance as well. Substance is what makes each song special. Substance can be a deep, profound message, or it can be a funny, gimmicky concept. It doesn't matter, so long as it's entertaining. Substance is what makes a song into a mini-drama, with meaning, conflict, and a distinct point of view. Substance is the part of the formula that separates the craftspeople from those in the Songwriter's Hall of Fame.

I know what you're thinking: "The songwriting greats don't use a formula. Formulas are for the uninspired, the unimaginative, or the unexceptional. They're what sneaky writers use to knock out a song with minimal effort." If this is your mindset, then the next section may come as a surprise. It offers some advice that might make your life just a little bit easier.

Embrace the "Form" in Formula

Not even the most original songwriters enter the writing process with an entirely blank slate. If the hit songwriting formula is one-half form and one-half substance, then sooner or later you have to decide what shape your song will take. Although it may be buried deep in their subconscious, almost all successful songwriters have a preferred form, or set of forms, that they use most often. This is a basic song structure that will serve as a blueprint for the song's development, provide for a reasonable amount of repetition, and give each section of the song the impact it needs.

The "form" in the formula doesn't detract from a great writer's individuality. It often becomes his or her stamp of identity. A great writer takes a standard song form and adapts it slightly to fit his or her musical style and by doing so creates a new variation that is unique and personal. If the songwriter then uses that customized song form repeatedly, it's merely an illustration of someone going with what works. Tiger Woods doesn't reinvent his swing on every hole. That doesn't mean that every shot is the same.

Once a songwriter has built the framework of a song, he or she can begin to add the creative inspiration: the substance that will be hung upon that basic structure. A brilliant lyrical concept or a surprising melodic twist will define the song, so that the form itself is hardly noticeable. No one cares that Stevie Wonder's "Living for the City" is a variation on a standard blues form. That's just the basic foundation. The substance of the song lies in the innovative chord changes, unforgettable melodic bridge, and the powerful social commentary of the lyric. That's what establishes the genius of Stevie Wonder.

Embracing the form in the formula just means that rather than resisting the idea of a standard song form, you study the various forms that the great songwriters have used and then personalize those forms to accommodate your own musical and lyrical style. This means finding a basic structure that works for you and then learning to make it your own.

The Prototype: Creating a Form

Just as the most cutting-edge film script is built on a three-act dramatic structure derived from the ancient Greeks, most song forms have their roots in older styles of music. Church hymns, English folk songs, African "call and response" chants, and the cowboy songs of the American West were all early influences in the development of American popular song structure. These old forms were condensed and combined to meet the needs of vaudeville and Broadway theater, the dance bands of the swing era, and the changing tastes of radio and television broadcast audiences, until finally settling into the forms most familiar today.

THE BLUES At its most basic, the blues is a standard twelve-bar form that essentially moves between the I, IV, and V chords. The original model is observable in almost any song by Bessie Smith or B. B. King—it went on to spawn the standard fifties rock 'n' roll song form, in songs like "Johnny B. Goode" and "Hound Dog." You can hear it in Memphis soul classics of the sixties like "Mustang Sally" or Santana's "Black Magic Woman." Led Zeppelin got pretty good mileage out of it in the seventies. In the eighties, it was adapted by Prince in "Delirious" and "Kiss." The blues are the bedrock of American music.

THE JAZZ STANDARD FORM This is the one to which most jazz songs from the thirties and forties adhere: an eight-bar statement of the "chorus," which is usually repeated, then an eight- or sixteen-bar bridge, then a return to a final eight-bar chorus. It's the foundation of old songs like "Moonglow," as well as classic Stevie Wonder songs like "You Are the Sunshine of My Life." It's timeless.

THE VERSE AND CHORUS This A-B form, a verse followed by a repeating chorus, seems to have descended largely from folk music, gospel music, and rhythm and blues, and it still survives in everything from punk rock to hip-hop. Today, it's usually altered a bit, as songs with just two alternating short sections feel a bit short for a modern audience. In the fifties, this form was the basis of hits like "Jailhouse Rock." Today, it's the structure behind most hip-hop records, with a rapped verse going directly into a sung hook.

THE A-B-C'S This is an obvious extension of the simple verse-chorus form. By the 1960s, writers were adding an additional section between the verse and chorus, to heighten the tension before going to the hook. Listen to how "I guess, you'll say/what can make me feel this way…" sets up the title line in the Temptations' "My Girl." This is a perfect "B" section, building momentum and drama before hitting the chorus. The A-B-C structure (verse, pre-chorus, chorus), and the A-B-C-D framework, which includes a bridge section, are the most common song forms for contemporary popular music, whether it's rock, pop, country, or urban.

The Winning Form: Selecting a Structure

While these are the most common song structures, there are many others that are recognizable, even to listeners without a musical background. Rock songs are often built on riffs—one instrumental line, most commonly a guitar part, which serves as the song's foundation. Urban music may use a James Brown–style vamp in which one basic groove runs through the entire song. Singer-songwriters frequently lean toward a simple series of verses, in which the hook usually appears as the first or last line of each stanza.

Clearly, there is no shortage of options from which to choose when selecting a song structure. If you find yourself getting lost in the possibilities, it's worth remembering the cardinal rule to almost all things artistic:

Form follows function.

Each form fits some genres better than others. Given that the fundamental functions of song form are to make the listener comfortable and to ensure that the song fits the format, you can immediately eliminate any song form not commonly used in the musical world for which you write. Urban writers can forget about the repeating-verse structure. Country writers can rule out a vamp form. A rock song is an awkward fit in the jazz standard mold.

Each form also fits some writers better than others. It's not an accident that a lyric-centered writer like Bob Dylan gravitates toward verse-verse songs, like "All Along the Watchtower." After all, this form leaves the most room for lyrics. Stevie Wonder uses the jazz standard form frequently, because it fits the jazz-oriented chord progressions that are an essential part of his style. The point of song structure is not only to make the listener comfortable but to make the writer comfortable as well. As you'll see later in this chapter, the challenges of creating the substance of a song are formidable. To allow you to focus all of your energy toward finding a compelling lyrical concept or discovering the perfect melodic hook, the song form needs to be an easy, effortless fit for your writing style. Like a good picture frame, it should naturally highlight your strengths as a writer, and help to camouflage some of your weaknesses.

Then, there's one other person to consider. You need to think about the artist who will sing your song, keeping in mind his or her strengths and stylistic preferences. When you're in the business of writing songs for others to sing, whatever song form you choose must make the artist comfortable. If you're writing a Celine-style ballad, you need a bridge with a dramatic high-note at the end of it. If you're writing for Miley Cyrus, you probably don't.

Finding a form that works means selecting something familiar to the audience and artist and suited to your own style and talent. It doesn't need to be innovative. You build on structure. The less noticeable it is, the better. Style comes in step two, as you start to make the form your own.

Making It Yours: Shaping a Song for Maximum Impact

So far, we've said that song structure should create a comfort zone for the listener, the writer, and the singer. Unfortunately, comfort is not enough. Comfort will give you something that sounds like a hit but not something that reacts like a hit. For that, you need to take your standard song structure and supercharge it for maximum impact.

This distinction, between a solid song structure and a solid song structure on steroids, is what differentiates writers who get songs recorded from writers who make hits. Any professional can create a song within the conventional framework. Consistent hit makers have learned how to adapt a standard song structure to give it new power. They make sure that each section of the song is a hook. They set up the song's key moments, so that those climaxes pay off in an emotionally satisfying way. Not only do they embrace the "form" in formula, but they take the form and make it better.

As an A&R person, I can usually recognize a song that's the work of an experienced hit songwriter only a few seconds into the introduction. At that early point, it's not a matter of quality. Rather, it's a matter of form and what's done with it. Novice songwriters use the introduction simply to set up the groove, with a keyboard or a guitar blandly playing the chords until the singer enters. Savvy songwriters use the opening section to establish a signature instrumental riff, or a melodic line. Even in those first few seconds, a hit songwriter is already getting his or her "hooks" in.

Smart songwriters never waste an opportunity to grab the listener—not just in the chorus, but in every section of the song. As soon as we hear the opening wah-wah guitar lick of "Let's Get It On," we're already captured. Almost every Elton John song, from "Your Song" to "Bennie and the Jets," opens with an immediately identifiable piano riff, which then reappears throughout the song. Listen to the Backstreet Boys' "As Long as You Love Me," and hear how Max Martin introduces a melody at the top of the song, played by a piano, then brings it back as a counterpoint to the melody in the chorus, then uses it again after the bridge, reprising the introduction.

We'll delve more into the role of "secondary hooks" in chapter eleven. At this point, what's important is to notice how an instrumental part, a recurring riff, or a counter-line to the melody can elevate each section of a song. By building hooks into each section, you make the song form more than just functional. Each hook pulls the listener deeper into the song.

It extends even further than that. In the best songs, each hook grabs the listener in the moment and also sets up the next hook.

Like any good joke, it's not only the punch line that creates the laugh. The setup and the payoff both are crucial. A song's introduction draws the listener in, but it also has to set up the verse. A bridge is a release from the verse and chorus structure that precedes it, but it's also a preparation for the final chorus. Each section has two functions: It must be a "payoff" for the section that preceded it and a "setup" for the section to come.

It all goes right back to the same principle that underlies the hit formulas themselves: different but not too different, fresh but long lasting, form and substance. The tension and release between two opposite forces coexisting is what creates the energy of a hit. In a well-structured song, the listener is pulled in by the rhythm of comfort and surprise, question and answer, conflict and resolution.

Ultimately, it takes contrast and momentum to generate impact. You can't grab an audience's attention simply by making each section of the song bigger than the previous one, with more instruments or background vocals. You'll get the most impact by ensuring that the verse, B-section, and chorus are each slightly different, with an unexpected lyrical twist, a melody that contrasts with what has come before, or a surprising change of instrumental texture.

Once you've mastered this process of drawing on a standard song structure and then maximizing the power of that structure by setting up hooks in each section, you will be able to create songs consistently that sound very much like hits. That's great news—but don't be fooled.

Form is only half of the formula. You've finessed a solid foundation on which to build, but you still haven't made a hit. You have to have something to say.

Making It Matter: Create a Concept

Comfort is good. Impact is better. Communication is best.

Communication requires ideas. If there is no idea, then even the most elaborate communication structure is rendered useless. Likewise, any songwriting formula requires more than just form. There has to be substance—an idea, thought, or story that you must express. Many songs that sound like hits have form but no substance. In most cases, we hear them, shrug our shoulders, and promptly forget they exist. To create a hit, you need to say something that matters. You need a concept.

What if I told you I was writing about a boy and a girl who fall in love? "Uh, how interesting..." you'd reply, as you quickly change the subject to something more absorbing, like the weather or the TV show you saw last night. I'm unlikely to intrigue anyone with a tale about two kids who fall in love.

On the other hand, if I told you that I was writing about a boy and a girl from two different backgrounds, who despite pressure from friends and family fall in love and fight desperately to stay together, then I might get your attention. I could be writing *Romeo and Juliet*—or "Leader of the Pack."

This is the power of a concept. A concept is not a vague feeling. It is a specific, compelling idea. Hit TV shows have concepts ("So there's this sponge, and he lives at the bottom of the ocean"); hit movies have them ("It's a gang of guys who rob banks, and they all get together for one last heist"); hit novels have them, too ("He's just a school kid, but he's also a wizard"). Certainly, hit songs have them, from "London Calling" to "London Bridge."

Unfortunately, most songs don't have them. Too often, songs communicate very little. With only three or four minutes to fill, it's too easy for a lazy or harried songwriter to fall back on a vague or predictable idea. When asked what his latest work is about, a songwriter will explain that "it's a love song," or a "party song." Sure. But what's the concept?

As I said in the previous chapter, songs can be about almost anything, whether it's the brotherhood of man ("We Are the World") or gold teeth ("Grillz"). There is no subject that can't be addressed effectively with a clever concept. If you say you're writing an ode to undying love and devotion, I'm probably not interested. If you have a concept like "When I'm Sixty-Four," I'm all ears. They key is to write about a subject that will be of interest to your targeted audience.

Creating a concept means finding an angle from which to tell a very specific story. If you're making a "mystery" movie, you can't make a movie about "mystery" in general. You have to make a movie about a specific situation that is mysterious. If you're writing a song about love gone wrong, you have to write about a specific set of characters in a particular situation. Love gone wrong is an idea. "Goodbye Earl" and "You Oughta Know" are concepts.

A concept is a big picture, seen through a small frame. Creating one forces you to find a very specific way of expressing a more general emotion or idea—and it's not easy. Nearly every writer has some song on the subject of "girl/boy, I need you so much," but only Sting wrote "Every Breath You Take." Devising a concept requires the same intensity of thought that an author would give to his or her novel, because a hit song concept is made up of the same qualities that define any good story.

A Little Conflict Never Hurts

Any concept is improved when it's built around a central conflict. The struggle could be physical, emotional, funny, or tragic. There are certainly plenty of familiar dilemmas that have served as the basis for countless hit songs:

- "I want you, but I can't have you."
- "Everyone tells me I shouldn't, but I have to do it anyway."
- "Why do you make me do what I know I shouldn't?"

While songs can exist without conflict ("My Girl," for example), they are always more dramatic when they contain opposing forces aligned against each other. This produces sparks of desperation, anguish, urgency, and all those elements that make a story compelling.

CREATING CONFLICT   Life does it for us every day. A quick reading of the newspaper will provide an endless variety of possible conflict to draw on: strong against weak, rich against poor, or man against nature. If that's too abstract, notice the person shouting into his cell phone on the bus. Something is at stake, and something has gone wrong. Conflict is not hard to find.

All you have to do to create conflict is to give the singer something he or she needs and then set an obstacle in the way. The greater the desire or need and the more challenging the obstacle, the more dramatic the struggle will be. If the concept for your song lacks energy or interest, this is an almost surefire way to fix the problem. Conflict is rarely dull.

On the other hand, conflict is not always fresh and original either. The generic conflicts that frequently show up in songs—"boy loses girl," "girl misses boy," "boy can't express what he's feeling"—have been the basis for hundreds of good, great, and pretty bad songs in the past. To make a concept unique, it takes something more.

It All Depends on Your Point of View

A point of view is simply a particular way of looking at the world that characterizes the person singing the song. Jimmy Jam and Terry Lewis weren't the first to write about a girl with an inattentive boyfriend. Yet "What Have You Done for Me Lately" had a unique attitude that brought the concept to life and made Janet Jackson a superstar. The difference between Sheryl Crow's "All I Wanna Do," Pink's "Get the Party Started," and Cyndi Lauper's "Girls Just Want to Have Fun" is not the concept, but the perspective. Each of them has an individual point of view that reinvigorates a fairly worn concept.

FINDING A POINT OF VIEW Any object looks different depending on the angle from which you view it. The trick to finding a fresh point of view is positioning. If you can define the age, the lifestyle, the tastes, and the nature of the artist for whom you want to write, then you can often find an original perspective on a subject, by seeing it through someone else's eyes.

In most cases, it's not all that important whether a song's point of view is angry or happy, amused or confused.

Any perspective can be commercially appealing, as long as it is sharply defined.

Indifference, apathy, and ambiguity don't translate well in a three-minute song. A hit is a kind of super-condensed drama, needing passion and energy for whatever angle it takes. Small, subtle emotions do not make hits. You need an attitude that's big enough to be noticed.

Think Big

Too many songwriters aim low. They try to write a "nice" little song that their friends will like, about a funny little thing that they heard someone say that made them feel just a little bit sad. Hit songwriters aim high. They want to write for a mass audience, about a subject that matters more than anything in the world to them. Not surprisingly then, hit writers pursue big concepts: "What the World Needs Now Is Love," "Beautiful Day," "Jesus Walks," "Enter Sandman."

Of course, not all hit songs are written to this oversize scale. Just as some hit movies are action blockbusters and some are quieter, indie films, no one size of song fits every artist or playlist. Songs like "Touch My Body" or "Keep Breathing" are far more intimate messages, delivered without much bombast. But even those songs are not introspective, obscure, or unemotional. A "big" song touches a universal chord and is not afraid to send a direct emotional message, whether it's with a whisper or a shout.

I remember being at a record label A&R meeting when someone was preparing to play a demo from a prospective pop artist. Right before the A&R person hit play on the stereo, the label president weighed in: "Just remember," he said to the group, "that a pop artist is someone who can sell twenty million records around the world. Keep that in mind as we listen."

That's thinking big.

The Songwriter's Challenge

Try asking yourself: Is this song idea one that 20 million people around the world could relate to? Is it possible to picture a stadium full of people singing along?

If it's not, then see if there's a way to "super-size it." Can you take an angle on the subject that is more universal? Can you increase the importance of what's at stake in the song, to make the emotion bigger or more dramatic? Can you alter the lyric so as to position the singer as a sort of spokesperson, a "voice" for his or her audience? Can you simplify the melody, to give it a more anthemic quality?

THE INSIDE TRACK

Shaping the Beautiful Disaster
Darrell Brown

SONGWRITER

Whether writing and producing for country superstars, working with blues legends like Willie Dixon and Steve Cropper, or helping to develop up-and-coming acts like The Daylights, Darrell Brown seeks to capture the immediacy of that first creative impulse and then refine the song in a deliberate step-by-step process. Brown is one of the writers of Keith Urban's "You'll Think of Me" and LeAnn Rimes's "Nothin' Better to Do." As he explains, it's a balancing act between form and substance that begins with the raw emotion but recognizes the audience's demand for hooks and the need to tailor a song to a specific artist.

DARRELL BROWN: A songwriter is a kind of emotional archeologist. You find something and then start to brush away the dust and you discover, "Oh, look—a piece of ceramic." You keep brushing away and you go, "Oh, look—it's a bowl." You keep brushing away and you go, "It's a bowl on top of a head. It's a statue. Oh, my God, it's the front of the door of a building." You never know how far it goes, or how big it gets. Our job is to delicately remove away what that song is and not try to distort it or make it into something it's not.

A lot of hit songs are just waiting to happen. You think of a phrase like "Blue Bayou"— if you're really sensitive you can hear what that song should be. Or, on another case, someone might hear that word "toxic" and say "Oh, I hate that word." Then later, someone like Cathy Dennis will say, "Oh, I know how to make that work." It's all about taking something ordinary and making it extraordinary.

It all starts with communicating an honest emotion. To show who you really are can be so powerful. Then you just have to raise the hook quality up. The more personal it is, the better. You think of Suzanne Vega's "Luka" or Dido's "White Flag"—the honesty is still there, but they made it a hit song. People really want to feel that they're not being lied to. When we hear honesty, that artist or songwriter is successful.

I think it was Bono who said that 60 percent of songwriting is getting ready to write, making tea, cleaning the house, and avoiding writing anything. Another 20 percent is getting all the chaos out in one big ugly blob. The last 20 percent is the fun part. That's the editing—moving things around, deciding what order you can put things in. There's no point in controlling the way that the chaos comes out. Just let it happen, without editing yourself. Then you can take that whole beautiful disaster and form it.

The key is to write where you are honestly and then take criticism in a good way. Most of the criticism is just, "Hey, can we move the furniture around a little? We're not going to take anything out, but can we move the chair here, and that there?" Sometimes you can find where a hook fits better in order to make a song more approachable.

I write for what's going on with me, just following my spirit and intuition. But I don't usually demo the song right away. Instead, I wait to see who's looking for material at the moment or going in the studio to record. Then, I look at my songs to see what I have. If I think a song is pretty close, I might just need to shape it a little, change that chord there, or that line for that artist or genre.

For instance, when we wrote "You'll Think of Me," Joe Cocker wanted to record it, but he wanted a bridge in the song. After we rewrote it, he decided not to cut the song—but now we had a bridge. Then when Keith Urban was looking at it, we adjusted some chords, and moved some things around again, and then we went in and did a demo of that. Everything kept changing and evolving.

As a songwriter, you have the song, but you also have the artist who's going to interpret it and you have to work with that. I look at it as if I'm an actor, Russell Crowe or Meryl Streep or whoever. You take that honest, personal emotion and then tailor it to a specific character. There may be something about the way a particular artist sings that you want to adjust to. You might find that changing one chord sounds more R&B or more country when you do the demo.

Can't Start a Fire...Without a Spark

The key to balancing form and substance is the order in which the two elements are addressed. Because it's easier to master, many songwriters begin with the form: functional chord progressions set into an eight-bar verse, pre-chorus, and chorus. Everything is perfectly calibrated to fit the target audience or artist. Once that much is in place, the capable craftsman then attempts to add a little substance, with a clever lyrical line or an unexpected melodic twist.

Hit makers work in reverse. For them, form follows substance. Inspiration leads, and discipline follows, giving structure and polish to the one big idea, that one honest emotion, that makes a song matter. The great songs always start with substance and then take shape from there.

Of course, shaping a song is no small undertaking. This is where hits are built—in a hundred small decisions, made line by line and chord by chord. As valuable as it is in determining direction, the formula is only the map. The next step is to take the journey.

Part Three
Write Your Own Hit

CHAPTER EIGHT

Creating a Hit Title

The Name Is the Game

There's a little book I keep on my desk, as a reminder of just how dangerous this business of writing can be. The book is called *Now All We Need Is a Title*, and it consists of anecdotes about the original and ultimately discarded titles of famous literary works. Did you know that *Of Mice and Men* was originally titled *Something That Happened*? Or that Margaret Mitchell's *Gone with the Wind* almost went by the name *Pansy*? When it comes to creating a successful novel, play, or song, there's a fine line between triumph and disaster. Very often, the line can be traced directly to the title.

Many experienced A&R people listen as much with their eyes as their ears. When working through the stack of demo recordings on their desks, they feel they can find the songs with hit potential simply by looking at the titles on CD covers. Most of the time, they're right. Much of what is good and bad about a song is evident from the title alone, and any experienced A&R person can immediately recognize the signs.

Just like the songs they represent, hit titles stand out. A title that's clever or surprising suggests a novel concept or a fresh point of view. A title that captures a bit of an attitude can give a new artist a little edge or reinvigorate the image of an established star. A lot can go wrong between coming up with a title and completing a song. Still, a strong title immediately puts the most important components of a hit song into place, by ensuring that there is a concept and a point of view that will make both the song and artist identifiable.

Conversely, songs with weak titles usually contain fatal flaws. A bland or vague title invariably reveals a song with little or no concept. An overused title shows a tired, unoriginal point of view. A title that could be sung by any type of artist will do nothing to define the artist who does record it. It's very difficult to turn a dull title into an exciting song, and most A&R people won't even give you a chance to try.

If you want to make a hit, the best place to start is by making a hit title. As soon as you accomplish this, much of the framework of your song will immediately fall into place. Similarly, if an already-finished song needs help, a new title will make a greater impact than anything else you could change. Whether you're laying the foundation at the beginning of the writing process, or trying to restructure a song that's not working properly, you have to get the title right.

What's the Big Idea?

Behind every great title is a great concept. Where there is a title like "Private Eyes," "Baby Got Back," or "Kiss from a Rose," there is an idea for a song. It's not hard to imagine what "You Don't Bring

Me Flowers" or "You've Lost That Lovin' Feelin'" is "about." These titles immediately lay a framework that keeps the lyric focused on one simple but specific concept. When you start with a hit title, the substance of a song is immediately apparent. After that, it's simply a matter of creating the form around that central idea.

A weak title is generic or vague. If you were to write a song about not dwelling on your troubles, you could title it "Don't Give Up." Or you could call it "When Times Are Tough." The former has been used at least a thousand times. The latter is neither a compelling image nor a specific idea. On the other hand, you could call the song "If You're Going Through Hell (Before the Devil Even Knows)." Immediately, an image is established, and the audience is given an angle from which the subject will be observed. The title is not so specific as to give away the entire premise: "If you're going through tough times, keep moving ahead." Yet, it's enough to whet our interest in the basic concept.

It's also enough to convey a certain attitude on the part of the singer. Is it any surprise that this is a country song? Just the presence of "the devil" is enough to signal that this artist has a certain down-home attitude. The phrase "if you're going through hell" leads us to think that the singer is something of a survivor. The title presents a point of view and casts an identity. Rather than opting for a predictable title like "Don't Give Up" (which tells us nothing about the personality of the singer), or something vague like "When Times Are Tough" (which tells us nothing of the singer's perspective), the writer has found a title that lays the groundwork for all that the lyric is trying to accomplish.

Will You Remember Me?

The whole purpose of song titles is to help consumers remember which song it was that they liked, so they can download it on iTunes later that evening. It follows then that a memorable title will be far more effective at selling copies of the song than a forgettable one. If listeners remember the tune but can't recall the title of your song, it's pretty doubtful that you'll be seeing much in the way of sales.

For the most part, people, places, stories, and songs are memorable for two reasons. Most often, it's a matter of simple repetition. We might forget a name or a face once or twice, but by the third time we've heard it or seen it, we find it suddenly lodged in our brain. Repetition is how we learn our lines for the high school play, how we teach our children, and how we remember the name of that guy we see every day at the office (unless we're musicians and just call everyone "Hey, man").

Resonance is the other key to memorability. Even if it happens only once, we hang on to those events that have significance in our lives: the day we signed the record deal, the day our child was born, or our wedding anniversary (we'd better remember that one). With enough repetition, almost anything can be memorable. With enough resonance, something can be memorable with no repetition at all.

As you've probably noticed when listening to the radio, the most common method of drilling a song into our consciousness is repetition. One important benefit to placing a title in the first line of the chorus is the possibility of repeating it more than once in each refrain. In songs like "I Want to Hold Your Hand" or "I Got

You Babe," the title is virtually the only lyric in the chorus. Part of the challenge of constructing a hit title is to understand how it will be placed in the chorus, to get the repetition it needs. One of my favorite hits from the disco era was "Enjoy Yourself," which simply proved that anything is memorable if you repeat it enough (in this song, it was "enjoy yourself," a mind-numbing forty-six times).

On the flip side, if your title line doesn't repeat often, it better be resonant. A major challenge for country writers is that the traditional country chorus often has the title falling in the last line, limiting the amount of repetition the title can have. Good writers compensate for this by making the title resonant. A strong country chorus sets up a situation and then allows the title line to provide the twist at the end—it's the twist that packs the punch. It might make you smile, or it might break your heart, but if it's done right, you'll remember it.

> *Well you took my wife*
> *And you took my kids*
> *And you took that life I used to live*
> *My pride, the pool, the boat, my tools, my dreams, the dog, the cat*
> *Yea, I think that's everything*
> *Oh, I almost forgot*
> *Do you want fries with that?**

Many modern rock songs also rely more on resonance than repetition when it comes to making the titles memorable. Songs like "Clocks" or "Chasing Cars" bury the titles in the middle of a chorus or somewhere in the verse. This works primarily because images of "closing walls and ticking clocks" or "chasing cars around our heads" are sufficiently striking to resonate without any repetition at all. Obviously, part of the appeal of these titles is that they disguise any attempt at being memorable, which gives them a certain kind of cool. Still, they do resonate with a listener, because they are iconic images or because they hold some element of surprise or mystery.

Just as important events in our lives resonate because of their emotional impact, titles resonate when they grab us unexpectedly and engage our emotions. They may tap into a memory ("Saturday in the Park"), confront us with a bold image ("Janie's Got a Gun"), intrigue us ("How to Save a Life"), or offer a sense of collective identity ("Born to Run").

What's the Long and Short of It?

Theories on the most effective length for a song title abound. Most successful pop songwriters set the ideal length at three words or fewer. Four words are fine, but five is pushing it, unless they are short words. Some people focus more on the number of syllables, noting that a three-word title like "Dance with Me" is actually shorter to say or sing than "Revolution" or "Apologize." Some writers focus solely on how a title sounds in the chorus; others try to visualize how it would look in print, on the Billboard Hot 100 chart (which is at least a fun exercise in wishful thinking).

When I was the creative director at Zomba Music, there was some confusion as to the exact title of Britney Spears's first single, which, had it included the entire hook, would have been quite long. Everyone finally settled on "...Baby One More Time." That opening ellipsis was a last-minute addition, probably to somehow allude to the slightly controversial "Hit me, baby" phrase, without having to actually say it. In the end, most listeners probably missed the effect of the extra punctuation.

All of which goes to show that there is no set length for a hit title. One- or two-word titles, like "One," "Yellow," or "Cry," have a certain iconic power. Three- and four-word titles seem to be the most common. I've often marveled at how Madonna's hits so often fit perfectly into three-word titles—from "Like a Virgin" to "Into the Groove" to "Ray of Light." The advantages of a short title are obvious: They're easy to remember, easy to sing, easy to understand, and easy to fit onto a *Billboard* chart. If you're looking for a quick answer to the question of length, keep your titles under four words.

Then again, don't be shocked if you see that limit violated, often by some of the best songwriters in the business. When it comes to creativity, not everyone plays by the same rulebook—which is precisely the point. Robert John "Mutt" Lange, the legendary writer/producer who's penned hits for everyone from Def Leppard to Shania Twain, is a champion of long titles: "When the Going Gets Tough, the Tough Get Going," "Get Outta My

Dreams, Get Into My Car," "I'm Not a Girl, Not Yet a Woman." The most recent advocate of the "bigger is better" theory for song titles is Brendon Urie, from Panic at the Disco, who has somehow managed to make phrases like "Lying Is the Most Fun a Girl Can Have Without Taking Her Clothes Off" into hit songs (although he seldom actually uses the title in the lyric).

Needless to say, *Billboard* managed to find room for all of those songs on the Hot 100 chart, despite their length. Writers like Mutt Lange and Brendon Urie recognize that while "short is sweet," longer can be stronger. If the primary function of the title is to stand out, then in a sea of three-word titles, a six-word title is almost sure to get noticed.

In fact, the first person who will notice a six-word title is likely to be the lead vocalist who has to sing it. You may have uncovered a clever phrase that will catch every A&R person's fancy, but first, the singer has to be able to coax it out of his or her mouth without becoming hopelessly tongue-tied. No matter how good they look on paper, the words have to fit a musical context—which is another matter altogether.

Does It Sing?

As the legendary Sammy Cahn once said, "Shakespeare would have been a lousy lyric writer. 'Love can laugh at locksmiths'? You can't sing 'locksmiths.' 'Locksmiths'? Forget it."

Songwriting and poetry are not the same things. After all the discussion of impact and identity, common language and the need for a twist, big concepts and memorable titles, the success or failure of a lyric often comes down to one simple question: Does it sing?

If you've been listening to the radio, or looking at the *Billboard* charts, while making your way through this chapter, you may have been wondering why so many songs with banal, clichéd titles seem to succeed, where other more interesting songs fail. How did "My Love" or "Tonight's the Night" or "Say You, Say Me" wind up at the top of the charts? There must be a thousand songs called "Forever." And yet, Chris Brown had a Top 10 hit with that title—and he probably won't be the last to use it.

More often than not, it comes down to how a particular phrase feels when it's sung. Because lyrics are a musical art, rather than a literary one, this one factor outweighs everything else. No matter how profound or moving the words might be, they have to feel good to sing.

Unfortunately, it's not easy to explain why singers are more comfortable with one combination of words than another. Certainly, much depends on what the words are saying and how they're saying it. Simple, direct emotional statements are much easier to sing than complex, calm, or measured ones. We can all recognize that "I Want to Hold Your Hand" sings considerably better than "I Would Like to Offer You My Hand." "I Want to Take You Higher" is better than "I Enjoy Elevating People's Sensibilities."

As a general rule, titles that speak directly to the listener ("Stop! In the Name of Love") are the most effective to sing. Titles that speak about the singer ("I Wish It Would Rain") are almost as strong. Titles that speak about a third person ("Eleanor Rigby") can work but are usually less immediately appealing. Titles directed toward a group of people in general ("People Get Ready" or "Give Peace a Chance") have to be very simple, like folk or gospel songs, to be sung effectively.

By nature, singing is much closer to shouting or public speaking than to writing or reading. It's not surprising then that many phrases that look fine on paper do not translate well into a musical phrase. It would be very awkward to shout, "How do you feel about our relationship?" "Do You Love Me?" works a lot better. For all its other attributes, music, especially popular music, is not an ideal medium for expressing subtle, complex ideas or mixed emotions. Urgency and passion, desire and longing—these are what the human singing voice was built to convey.

Even so, not every simple, direct phrase sings well. Someone once sent me a song called "Bunt." It's simple, all right. It's direct. It could be emotional, I suppose, given the right context. Yet I suspect even the most gifted vocalist would struggle to make that particular word sing. Most often, whether a word works in a musical context is determined by the sound of the word itself. It's a mystery of vowels and consonants.

Most singers can easily attest to the value of vowel sounds—the *ahs*, *ees*, *is*, *ohs*, and *ooh*s are the sounds that allow voices to open up and show what they can do. Sounds like *er*, *uh*, and *eh* tend to shut the voice down. Consonants can't really be sung at all, but they add rhythm and a percussive quality when used effectively. All of these sounds—the open vowels, the closed vowels, and the consonants—are necessary, and each has its appropriate use in a melodic phrase. Like wind in a sail, a proper match of melody and vowel sounds will make a phrase sing.

Herein lies the mystery. Some rules, like trying to match open vowels on long notes, and closed vowels on shorter ones, can be helpful. Trying to work certain explosive consonant sounds, like *guh*s, *duh*s, or *buh*s, into percussive phrases is usually better than repeating *s* sounds. Nevertheless, the ability of great songwriters to create phrases that sing defies complete explanation. I don't know how Elton John turns phrases like "Captain Fantastic and the Brown Dirt Cowboy" into melodies. That's why it's so interesting to hear him do it.

I do know that awareness is the first step to making titles sing. Listen to the way the vowels fall when you say the words. Notice how the sound of the words affects the melody. Is there a word that's stopping the momentum of the phrase? Is there something that the singer is struggling to sing correctly? You need to focus on both a lyric's meaning and its sound. Above all, always respect the two ironclad rules of songwriting:

Melody takes precedence. Always. Over everything.

And:

If the title feels a little awkward, it is.

Even if the title does exactly what it is supposed to do, even if it captures all the things you've ever wanted to express, even if it came to you in a dream or a fit of creative inspiration—if it doesn't sing, the words must change. That's why they call it songwriting.

Five Favorite Title Tricks

Given all this discussion of concept, repetition, resonance, vowels and consonants, and the primacy of melody, it might seem difficult to ever come up with a title that looks and sounds like a hit. It's not. A professional songwriter usually has whole books full of title ideas. They won't all be hits, of course, but many of them might be, even if not for that particular writer. It's always a strange feeling when a song with the same title as yours shows up on the radio. There's a mixture of simultaneous triumph ("See, I knew that was a great title!") and despair ("There goes another million-dollar idea.").

Just like any other craft, songwriting has its share of tricks. These are quick and easy techniques for spurring creativity and focusing ideas. In the interest of getting off to a good start, here are Five Favorite Title Tricks that should help to set you on the road to a hit.

Catch a Phrase

It's like catching a wave, only a little less exciting. To find a title that feels comfortably familiar, speaks in a common language, and has resonance with your audience, simply grab a phrase from everyday speech. This could be a common phrase ("I Heard It

Through the Grapevine"), a bit of slang ("Get Crunk"), or a new brand name gaining popularity ("Air Force Ones"). For extra points, flip the phrase around somewhere toward the end of the chorus to change or enlarge the meaning.

Double Up

The clever play on words, usually with a double meaning, is a particular favorite of country writers, who wield their words like double-edged swords. "Nothin' On But the Radio" is a clever pun that makes you smile when you get it. "She Let Herself Go" takes a phrase and uses two meanings to show two sides of the situation. Rock writers also like to have a little fun with this kind of word-play, in songs like "Love in an Elevator." It's a smart trick, all right, but be forewarned: Sometimes it's a little too smart. Nashville writers love to laugh about titles like "I Still Miss You Baby...But My Aim Is Getting Better," or "Please Bypass This Heart." Used too freely, double meanings raise a red flag that reads, *Caution. Songwriter at Work.*

Picture This

Nothing resonates deeper and faster than one great image. From "Stairway to Heaven" to "Free Bird" to "Your Body Is a Wonderland," a vivid image, a simile, or a metaphor works on several levels at once. It engages the listener on a subliminal emotional level, by the beauty of the imagery. At the same time, it engages the listener's mind in trying to discover what the image might mean. Lyrics are not poetry, but lyrics do use many poetic elements.

Shock Me

Sometimes, it also doesn't hurt to have the touch of a tabloid journalist. There's no denying that in the world of entertainment, a little outrage or scandal can take you a long, long way. From "Baby Let's Play House" for Elvis, to "Sympathy for the Devil" for the Rolling Stones, to "Not Ready To Make Nice" for the Dixie Chicks, there's always been value in a little shock.

The Songwriter's Challenge

It's hard to beat the TV or radio talk shows for digging up the most outrageous subjects, the wildest fetishes, or the personalities most prone to misbehave. Take a moment to watch or listen, and see if you can find:

1. A political issue rife with hypocrisy and corruption. Try writing a "Sign 'O' the Times" or "Masters of War."

2. A public figure ripe for ridicule. Maybe we need a song like the Pet Shop Boys' "I'm with Stupid."

3. A segment of society suffering injustice. Who could hold back Public Enemy's "Fight the Power"?

4. A subject formerly off-limits. Think "I Kissed A Girl."

Don't be shy—you generate controversy by articulating what no one else is quite willing to say. Pushing the right buttons is sure to get you noticed.

Title the Album

Tom Nichols, the writer of "Have You Ever Been in Love" for Celine Dion, revealed to me that one of his secrets is to try to write the title cut of an album. That just means understanding the artist for whom you're writing the song and thinking about where he or she might be in his or her career or personal life. Is the artist just married or going through a well-publicized breakup? Is he or she embracing a social cause or firing a manager? Is this a debut album, a comeback, a concept piece, or a venture into a new area? Once you've decided where the artist is, or should be headed, it's a simple case of finding the phrase that sums it all up. Titles like "Control," "A New Day Has Come," "American Idiot," or "Welcome to the Black Parade" come with an artist identity and direction built in.

Every Song Has a Story
Sharon Vaughn

SONGWRITER

With country classics like "My Heroes Have Always Been Cowboys," "Out of My Bones," and "Lonely Too Long" to her credit, as well as pop songs that appear on seven recent Number One albums around the world, legendary songwriter Sharon Vaughn is a master at blending imagery, concept, and a perfect match of melody and words to create songs that define an artist. For her, it starts with a knowledge of the vernacular of the genre in which she's working (as she puts it, "without that, you're dead in the water") then relies on a blend of discipline and intuition to tell a story that takes the listener on a fully realized journey, with a beginning, middle, and end.

SHARON VAUGHN: So much of what I do came by way of classic songwriters like Jules Styne, Cole Porter, or Irving Berlin. The first music I remember listening to was the standards—"Guess I'll Hang My Tears out to Dry," "Deep Purple," "You've Changed." Because most of those writers came from the theater, the songs are very visual and evocative. They had to set up characters and setting. They start with that first line

174

and they carry that common thread until they wrap it up with a neat little bow at the end. It's the hardest way to write, but it's the most compelling.

It's very challenging to write about concepts. You have to be open and disciplined at the same time. When someone plays a melody that speaks to me, the melody will insist on what it wants to say. If you try to force the wrong title on a song, it just won't work. You don't want to write some happy little jig for someone who's bleeding. But once you start a song, and you settle on a lyrical concept, then you have to commit completely and see it through. I think that if I have a talent, it's for knowing how to make a song stay the course and not lose itself.

A lyric has to sing. That's huge. If you can't sing it, you have to change it. There's no sense in stumbling. My acid test is "How would Bonnie Raitt sound singing this?" To me, she fondles a word before it gets out of her mouth, and that's why I believe every syllable she sings. So I work really hard at that. The words have to feel true to the person singing them.

If I had the choice, I'd have the artist there in the room the whole time I'm writing. I want to know what their life is like and hear how they sound saying the words. I'm developing a new artist now, and he has to trust me not to put false words in his mouth. So sometimes I'll ask him, "Would you say this? Are you comfortable saying it that way?"

> For me, the most important lines are the first line of the song and the line just before the title. That setup line for the title—that's the tricky one. That's where you earn your stripes. I'm so disappointed when people just throw a title away. You need to beef it up. It's like making a terrific stock and cooking something in it, or just cooking the thing in water. You have to work on that first line, because it better knock your socks off— and then you have to make sure you set that title up.

Titles Last

With a few good title tricks up your sleeve, it shouldn't be so hard to come up with a few possible phrases to build a song around. Inspiration can come from anywhere—television, an advertisement, an overheard conversation, or a poignant memory. Make sure to keep a notebook handy, and jot down a running diary of words, ideas, snippets of dialogue, or catchy new slang. Then, before the writing process begins, take a quick look to see if there's an idea that might fit your mood or the project at hand. As long as you settle on a clever concept that's both memorable and comfortable to sing, you've got a solid foundation from which to begin the more challenging work of writing a song.

Unless, of course, you're working in reverse. As you may have already found, that's a lot more difficult. Those of you who have been using the principles in this chapter to retitle an already-finished song probably have discovered just how truly vexing the name game can be.

I learned this lesson early on—the first time I had one of my own songs recorded. When I arrived at the studio for the vocal recording session, I was greeted at the door by the A&R man, who began by assuring me how much everyone liked my song. "All except for the title," he added. "That definitely needs to change."

Apparently, it had never occurred to the A&R decision makers that the title was the basis for the whole song. Now, only minutes before the artist was to arrive at the studio, I was being asked to go back to square one and find a way of expressing the same idea in words that weren't merely different but better. In the end, after killing several hours and two notepads, I did mange to come up with an idea that was indeed different. Whether it was better remains open to question.

Changing the title of a finished song can feel nearly impossible, especially if you want to leave the rest of the lyrics intact. It's like changing the cornerstone of a building while it's still standing. Given the difficulty of the endeavor, it hardly seems worth trying.

Except that I have this small book on my desk, reminding me of all the now classic movies, plays, and songs that were saved only by a last-minute title change. In most cases, it would be impossible to argue that the song would have had the same success under the original name. After all, the working title of "Yesterday" was "Scrambled Eggs."

If you sense that your title is limiting the song's effectiveness, you can't afford not to go back to the drawing board one more time.

As difficult as they may be to find, the right three or four words can transform a song from forgettable to immortal.

Do you remember your high school fight song? I barely knew mine, even when I was in high school—and neither did anyone else. The only thing the crowd at the football game seemed to know was the title (which was the opening line) and the tune.

That's true of a lot of songs. Over time, much of the detail work done by songwriters fades away. What remains, inevitably, is the title and melody. Finding the right title is half the battle. In chapter nine, we'll turn to a new and bigger challenge: setting those words to music.

Making Hit Tunes

That Mysterious Melody

At this point, there are probably some angry track producers and lyricists still smarting over the Golden Rule of songwriting from the previous chapter: Melody takes precedence. Always. Over everything.

"Why should it? People like songs for beats just as much as melodies," the programmer/producer will argue. "Songwriting is all about having something to say," retorts the lyricist.

The truth is this: Music is melody. Even within a beat, there is melodic structure—a variance in pitch between the kick and snare, or two different congas, and a recognizable pattern of repetition and variation. Chord progressions work when each note in a chord leads melodically to the next chord. If you recite a line from a favorite song, your voice will inevitably catch some of the inflections and rhythm from the original melody. It's very hard to say the words "yesterday all my troubles seemed so far away" without a pause after "yesterday" and a slightly longer inflection on the word "far." The melody is how we remember the words.

For traditionalists, songs are defined as words and melody. Anything else—drum patterns, chord progressions, instrumental parts—is all part of the arrangement, not the actual song. In the modern music industry, this point of view no longer predominates. Today, most A&R people, producers, and writers consider a song to be made up of the "track" and the "topline." The track, usually created by a composer who is also a producer, will provide the musical "bed" for the song, including chord progression, rhythm pattern, and arrangement. Picture the whole final mix of the song, but with all of the vocals muted. That's the track.

This raw musical idea will then be given to a topline writer, usually a singer, who will add the vocal line (melody and lyrics). Often the process is so impersonal that the topline writer may never meet the track writer at all. It is a division of labor not so different than the one between a traditional composer and a lyricist, except that the responsibility for creating the melody has shifted. In most cases, the topline writer, rather than the composer, is responsible for creating the primary vocal line.

As we'll see later in our interview with the production team Stargate, this new way of defining a song doesn't mean that composers no longer care about melody. In fact, a guitar line or a string part could be one of the most melodic and identifiable parts in a song. Successful track writers try to embed these melodic ideas into the track itself to inspire the topline writer and to shape how the melody will fit with the music. They know from experience that no matter what bells and whistles they might throw into the mix, the primary importance of the lead vocal line is indisputable. No one walks away whistling the percussion part. There's nothing more valuable than a hit melody.

Unfortunately, there's also nothing more mysterious. Chord progressions can be analyzed by the fundamental rules of harmony. Rhythm is primarily a matter of mathematical subdivisions. Melody defies easy analysis. As we've already noticed, there are a few general principles that can be applied, particularly the concept of repetition and variation. Still, if you want to know precisely why the melody of "I Say a Little Prayer" gets in your head and won't leave, you'll find yourself hard-pressed for a satisfying explanation.

No one can tell you precisely how to write hit melodies. However, it is possible to discover specific strategies that will improve your melodic writing. This chapter is where many of the general principles of comfort and surprise, form and substance, and tension and release are given a very practical application. Once you clearly understand how melody functions within different genres of music, you can create vocal lines that are simple and accessible and yet tell a story that will keep listeners anticipating the next "twist." Then you can go further and apply those same ideas to other elements in the song, making your whole track more melodic. It might not turn you into Burt Bacharach. Then again, if it could, this would be a much more expensive book.

Everybody Sing!
Keeping It Simple

Oh no. It's the "simple" thing again. We already know that simple is good, as it provides the listener with the comfort of the familiar. We also know that simple is hard, because it requires stripping away the superfluous. But what does "simple" mean when it comes to melody? Does it mean that everything must be dumbed down to a singsong, nursery school tune?

Well, maybe—if you're writing for children. Going back to our cardinal rule in chapter five, a simple melody is one in which the form perfectly matches the function. It does what needs to be done, without any wasted ornamentation, detours, or acrobatics. Think of the absolute economy of "Let It Be." It suits the specific genre, fits the singer, and encourages the audience to sing along.

Melody and Genre

Before you can write effectively in a particular style, you have to understand how melody functions in that genre. In most traditional pop or adult contemporary songs, the melody is the engine that provides the emotional and dramatic energy. Alternatively, most country songs derive much of their emotion from the lyric but require a chorus melody that lends itself to vocal harmonies. In R&B and hip-hop, most chorus hooks are built on a call-and-response form that goes back to gospel music. Meanwhile, modern rock songs often strive for an almost classical kind of catharsis, with melodies that build carefully throughout the verse and B-section and then release with a vengeance in the chorus.

Once you understand the function, it becomes obvious that the melody needs to fit within certain parameters of range, rhythm, and repetition. If pop songs use melody as their primary source of dramatic power, then those melodies are likely to be wide in range, with plenty of peaks and valleys and large leaps from one note to the next. Conversely, if country melodies are built to harmonize easily, then they will usually have a limited range, easy step-by-step movement between pitches, and not a great deal of rhythmic syncopation. Traditional R&B melodies have two melodic hallmarks: The hook functions almost like a background vocal part, with a small range, frequent repetition, and plenty of vocal harmonies, while the lead vocal response will be dramatic, with surprising jumps in register and much more ornamentation than would be found in country or pop. An "emo" song will invariably have some high notes in the chorus to push the singer to the top of his or her register and generate the required emotional release, while singer-songwriter material, like "Bubbly," will avoid those peaks, keeping the singer within a comfortable range and using simple melodic phrases to maintain the sincere, low-key vibe.

Keeping your melody within the limits of the genre serves both the singers and the audiences who sing along with them. A hip-hop melody, like Cassie's "Me & U," has a very limited range, which allows a young artist with an untrained voice to deliver it effectively and a teenage audience to join in. Alternatively, the melody to Kelly Clarkson's "Since U Been Gone" has a wide range, tailor-made for a singer with a big voice and an audience that likes a dramatic hook. Older, classic rock songs like "Jump" or "We Will Rock You" are almost chant-like in their simplicity— they're one step beyond football cheers. That's because they're meant to be sung by rock stars in stadiums, for a largely male audience.

> "Simple" means understanding what's needed, what the limits are, and what the audience wants, then doing just that. It means not doing too much.

No matter what the genre, the identifying characteristic of a simple melody is economy. It uses as much rhythm, repetition, and range as the genre can accommodate and no more.

The Songwriter's Challenge

Looking at melodies from the genre in which you write, let's analyze how melody functions within that particular musical style. Pick five hit songs within your market, and put those melodies to the test:

1. Is the range of the melody wide (over an octave and a half) or narrow (within an octave)?

2. How much melodic repetition is used within each section of the song? How similar are the melodies in the verse, pre-chorus, and chorus?

3. How much vocal harmony is used in the chorus? Are the harmonies used to support the primary melody (usually a parallel line above or below the main melody) or in counterpoint to the primary melody (as in a call-and-response)?

4. Is the chorus rhythmically simple (quarter notes, half notes, and whole notes) or more complex (eighth and sixteenth notes)?

5. Where is the highest note in the melody? Does it correspond to the peak emotional moment?

When you're working on this Songwriter's Challenge, don't get hung up on the fact that the five songs may differ widely in some respects. If you've narrowed the genre sufficiently (that is, you're comparing Rihanna to Fergie, and not to Avril Lavigne or Fall Out Boy), then you'll start to see some general patterns emerge, even if there are plenty of exceptions from one song to another. Once you have a clear picture of what a successful melody sounds like in your style of music, it's time to see how your tune measures up.

The Songwriter's Challenge

Using a song from your own catalog, apply the same analysis that you used in the previous exercise. How does your song match up against other songs in your genre?

It's natural for any song to fall "outside the norm" in one or two areas. But if your melody seems entirely at odds with what is typical for your market, it might be time to do some trouble-shooting:

1. If the range of your melody is too wide, can you sing a vocal harmony line that fits underneath the lead vocal? Try making that part the primary melody.

2. If your song is too narrow in range, try the same approach but in reverse. Is there a higher harmony part above the lead vocal that could become the actual melody of the song?

3. To break up a melodic pattern that repeats one too many times, try starting the repetitive phrase a half a beat earlier or later or beginning on a different note. Just a slight variation will force you to

follow the old phrase with a new melodic line.

4. Rhythmic activity is easy to add or subtract, but the lyrics will have to change. Try singing the melody like a jazz "scat" singer, using percussive syllables instead of the lyric. Once you've found the right rhythmic feel for the phrase, go back and make the lyrical adjustment. Listen to how Randy Bachman injected a simple "b-b-b-baby" to give "you ain't seen nothing yet" a little rhythmic punch.

Keep It Moving: Building the Story

Simple is great. Dull is not. While it's a good general rule to aim for a melody with as few notes as possible, you still have to keep things interesting—not only in the chorus but in every section of the song. Any moment without a memorable melody is wasted space. Whether it's in the introduction, the bridge, or an instrumental solo, listeners demand a focal point that constantly holds their interest.

Too many songwriters ration out their good melodies, not wanting to waste their best stuff on a bridge or an intro and justifying a dull verse in the name of "dramatic build." They apply the principles of melodic construction, repetition, and surprise to the chorus but suspend them in the B-section, relegating those eight bars to function as a stepping stone to the real hook that will follow.

In fact, dramatic build is created the same way in a song as it is in a movie script. In a good piece of screenwriting, each scene has its own arc, its own tension, and its own resolution. More important, each scene's resolution leads to the next scene, where the pattern of tension and resolution begins again.

In the same way, a verse melody usually begins with an opening statement of the central melodic idea. The next phrase either repeats or echoes the first idea, raising the stakes and building the tension. A third phrase will offer a shadow of the opening idea, but now with a change, altering the rhythm or jumping to an unexpected note. This creates a conflict, requiring resolution. For the listener, this becomes the peak moment of that section as we wait to hear how this tension in the melody will be released. That small climax should then resolve into the final line of the verse and lead us into the B-section, so that the pattern can begin again—repetition, surprise, and a complication that finally leads to an ultimate resolution in the chorus. The verse of the Motown classic "Just My Imagination" is a good example of this traditional but timeless approach.

This is the challenge of the A-B-C (verse–pre-chorus–chorus) form. Each section stands on its own but also sets up what follows. You want to get to the chorus, but there should also be memorable melodies in each section, leading up to that main hook. The key is to keep things moving. The natural rhythm of theme, variation, and resolution will carry your melody forward through the course of a four- or eight-bar journey. On a larger scale, you can utilize those same ideas of repetition and contrast to make sure that each melodic idea prepares a new surprise in the next section.

The Songwriter's Challenge

To create the proper setup, sometimes you must work backward. Using one of your own songs, see if you can improve the chorus melody just by changing what comes before it.

1. If the chorus is made up of long notes, then the B-section can have a more active melody. If the chorus is melodically busy, then try to make the last line of the B-section simple and spare.

2. If the first line of the chorus is the title line or a peak melodic moment, make sure that there's ample space around it. Try putting at least one beat of silence right before the downbeat of the chorus.

3. On your way into the chorus, an ascending or descending melody will add a sense of motion and momentum. A melody with less movement, but a little extra repetition, will add tension. Experiment to see which gives your chorus greater impact.

Listen to the give and take of the melody in Daughtry's "It's Not Over": the gradual build of the verse as it moves up in register; the contrast between the long, held notes and the short quick phrases; and the way the rhythmic push of "I'll try to do it right this time around" naturally sets up the dramatic, sweeping title line. As impressive as the production and arrangement are on this record, all the momentum is built into the melody itself. It relentlessly pulls the listener along from line to line, and section to section.

At his induction to the Songwriter's Hall of Fame, the Lovin' Spoonful's John Sebastian shared some advice he received from his mother, when he first began the challenge of songwriting:

Tell a story, the way you would tell it to someone who was genuinely interested.

That's good advice when it comes to lyrics, but it's equally good advice for creating a melody. If you think of your melody as a story, the intuitive storytelling ability that is part of human nature will lead you to a balance of tension and resolution, setup and payoff. Each section of a song is like the chapter of a book, a story within a larger story, that must have its own dramatic arc but also must keep the momentum moving toward the final destination. Naturally, every listener wants to get to the chorus, just as every reader is eager to see how the novel turns out. Still, getting there should be half the fun.

Melody Is Where You Find It

One way to be sure that each section has something of melodic interest is to broaden the definition of melody. It's not just what the singer sings. A melody can be a bell line, a horn lick, a guitar arpeggio, or even a spoken line.

An interesting question has been raised in certain copyright infringement cases as to whether it's possible to copyright a drum pattern. In some instances, the courts have ruled that a drum part or other rhythmic element can be protected when it's the featured element of a song. In the absence of any other identifiable hook, it essentially becomes what the audience recognizes as the melody. For example, if a cowbell is the only pattern being played, or at least the most identifiable, then the cowbell part is the song. In other words, melody is where you find it.

This can be particularly important in hip-hop, where the "music" might be little more than a drum pattern and a rap, neither of which is inherently melodic. A hip-hop hook could be anything from a synth line ("Nuthin' But a 'G' Thang") to a chant ("Party Like a Rockstar"). Nevertheless, the same basic principles of melody hold true. Even the most street-oriented rap record will benefit from simple but well-constructed "melodic" elements (whether it's a bass line, a string part, or a percussion part) in each section of the song.

For this reason, smart producers and arrangers try to make every instrumental part into a melodic element. Why have a guitarist just strumming chords if he or she could play the progression in a way that would create a counter-melody to the sung vocal line? Why have a bass line simply outline the chord progression if it could be a pattern that would become a hook by itself?

Every part that you add to the production can introduce a new melodic idea, reinforce an already existing melody, or create a counter-melody to the primary vocal line.

It shouldn't take a producer or an arranger to make your song sound like a hit. If you listen to Paul Simon's guitar part on "The Sounds of Silence," you'll hear all the elements of a complete arrangement. He knew that the counter-lines, arpeggios, and rhythmic motion were integral elements of the song. The guitar riff that drives "Whole Lotta Love" isn't an arranging choice. Without it, there's hardly a song at all. The only people who draw a distinction between "arrangement," "production," and "songwriting" are songwriters and musicians. Regardless of whether it comes from a guitar, a vocalist, or a cowbell, the casual listener simply hears the melody and is drawn in.

The Songwriter's Challenge

Choose a song from your catalog that you've already recorded or performed live.

Looking at the arrangement of the song, identify each of the musical elements (guitar, bass, piano, background vocals, strings, horns). Excluding the lead vocal and the drums, how is each part creating a new melody, supporting the lead vocal line, or providing a counterpoint to the primary melody? Could the guitar play something more melodic than a straight strumming part? Does the bass do more than just anchor the chord progression? Can the string or horn lines create a contrasting melody to the vocal, rather than blending into the harmonic progression?

Try to inject at least one melodic idea into each element of the arrangement.

THE INSIDE TRACK

Making Melodies Your Own
Stargate
SONGWRITERS

Few writing-production teams have used their signature melodic sound to better advantage than Stargate, the Norwegian production team made up of Mikkel Eriksen and Tor Erik Hermansen. Since coming to America in 2005, they've run up a remarkable string of chart-topping singles that include Beyonce's "Irreplaceable," Ne-Yo's "So Sick" and "Sexy Love," and Rihanna's "Unfaithful," "Don't Stop The Music," and "Take A Bow." Stargate songs are inevitably simple, uncluttered, and centered on an immediately identifiable melodic idea.

TOR: It's taken us a long time to get to our own style, our own sound. We've studied all the great ones: Stevie, Prince, Jam, and Lewis. But when we came to America, what people picked up on were the melodies that were unique, that came from us, from the experience that they don't have. We mix in Scandinavian folk notes that are within us, along with music that isn't typically American, like Depeche Mode and those kinds of harmonies. It's when we started finding our inner voice that we found what's unique about ourselves.

MIKKEL: It's great when you get to the point where you can trust your own language. Then you can do what comes natural to you. That's what works.

TOR: For years, I was always listening to other people's melodies and thinking, "What's great about these melodies that ours don't have?" At that point, we were nowhere—other people were getting all the hits. I was always trying to pick up what they were doing. Finally, the moment we let go of all that and found our voice, that's when it started to happen.

MIKKEL: It's like any art form, like a painter. It's when you find your own expression that you can become great.

Interestingly, despite the melodic nature of their music, Stargate do not usually write the vocal melody and lyrics of their songs. Instead they create the track and then hand the musical composition over to the industry's leading topline writers, like Ne-Yo, Taj Jackson, and Johnta Austin, to create the vocal melody and lyric. Nevertheless, the venture remains a collaborative effort, with many of the musical ideas inherent in Stargate's tracks often serving as the basis of the vocal melody.

MIKKEL: We do put a lot of melody in the track. We don't quit until we have some kind of melodic idea in the music—not just a chord progression or a beat, but a strong melodic core in the music.

TOR: On the Lionel Richie song ("I Call It Love"), I remember creating that melodic part that opens the song. The interesting thing is, at the end of the chorus, Taj (Taj Jackson, the co-writer of the song) was singing that same melody we were playing in the introduction. When we did "So Sick," Ne-Yo delivered a groundbreaking lyric, but again, in the chorus he's singing the melody that we're outlining in the track. On the other hand, "Irreplaceable" is an example of where Ne-Yo came up with a melody that we would have never thought of. Because that was more of a guitar-led track, it didn't really have such a defined melody when we gave it to him.

MIKKEL: Our favorite melodies are when the topline writer hears an instrumental part in the track that sparks his or her interest and then picks up on that and develops it.

TOR: When you start out as a writer, sometimes you're kind of afraid to define the melody. I look at it like making a painting. There's a Norwegian artist named Edvard Munch—what's special about him is that he has these very strong lines. He was never afraid to make a line. He's not putting a dot here and there—it's very defined. I think it's the same in music. Don't be afraid to put a melody on there, with a start and a finish—something that's very clearly defined.

The shape of those melodic lines is something to which both Mikkel and Tor pay significant attention. While neither would describe their approach as formulaic, they readily acknowledge that certain patterns are more consistently effective than others.

TOR: Melodies that work have a lot in common. I saw an interview once with Sir George Martin. He was saying that, for some reason, all of the best pop songs have two repetitive lines in the beginning of the chorus, then a climax, then a resolution. I was like, "You gotta be crazy."

Then I started to listen to different, big songs, and I realized, "He's right." You could easily find a lot of exceptions. But I looked at the songs that we did that worked, and it dawned on me that they had the same formula. We just didn't know what we were doing. Like in "Irreplaceable," "You must not know 'bout me, You must not know 'bout me..." there's the two lines that repeat.

MIKKEL: The other key is relatively straight melodic lines with a twist in the end. Don't let the melody go up and down and all over the place—you want progressions. Listen to the hook of "Unfaithful"—it has that shape to it. "I don't wanna hurt him..." is all around the same note, then "anymore" is the twist at the end. Then the next line echoes it—"I don't want to..." is fairly flat, then "take away his life" has the intervals in it.

We're not the ones who come up with those melodies, but we can maybe steer the topline writers in the right direction or recognize that structure when we hear it. It helps make the creative decisions easier. It's improved our strike rate just knowing what we're doing.

TOR: You learn to recognize when something is in the right parameters. It doesn't mean that it's a hit record, or even a good record. It's just another tool in your toolbox to help you make good decisions in the writing process.

Because many songwriters are accustomed to constructing melodies intuitively, by singing along with a chord progression or finding a musical phrase that corresponds with an existing lyric idea, it can be eye-opening to understand the thought and care that hit makers like Stargate bring to melodic construction. What looks like a natural talent is actually the result of considerable study and research. In the end, melody is too important to be left solely to inspiration and instinct. As Tor explains:

TOR: We now really understand the importance of a great topline melody, in order for a song to go all the way. When we have a great musical track, we think, "This has the potential to be something special." But you never know if it's special until you have that topline melody. Sometimes you're let down, and sometimes you're blown away.

The Science of Sounding Natural

The craft of melodic construction requires more than just improvising vocal lines over a preexisting track. You'll need a thorough understanding of the way melody functions within a specific genre, as well as how one melodic idea relates to the other, to create a compelling musical journey. The process doesn't end with the primary vocal line but extends to each element of the musical arrangement, using melodic ideas to engage the listener at every point.

For all the changes that have transformed popular music over the past century, one thing remains true: The tune is always the driving force of the song. Melody is to music as plot is to drama. So it's not surprising that much of what sounds effortless in performance is the result of endless hours and discipline, of paring each line down in search of the perfect balance between functionality, economy, and beauty. Picture the old Tin Pan Alley composer, painstakingly plunking his melody out note by note on the piano— no chord progression, no drum track, no lyric. That's the true test of any melody, and you won't pass it without plenty of trial and error and a willingness to rewrite until you've found the simplest and best solution.

CHAPTER TEN

The Rhythm of a Hit

Songwriting for the Rhythm Nation

So if melody is that important, where is all of it?

Listening to the radio today, you're unlikely to be overwhelmed by the number of beautiful melodies wafting through the speakers. On certain stations, it might be hard to hear much melody at all. How could you, when all you're hearing is drums?

Even if it's in short supply, melody remains the most defining element of a song. But in most current hits, it's certainly not the most prominent element. Fifty years after the teenagers of *American Bandstand* immortalized the phrase "It's got a good beat—and you can dance to it," we've all become slaves to the rhythm.

When it comes to today's Top 40 radio, a compelling, dynamic rhythm is an essential element in creating a hit record.

To be sure, rhythm is everywhere. There is rhythm in melody, in chord progressions, and even in a good lyric. However, that's not the rhythm we're talking about—at least not in this chapter.

Here, we're going to explore what a hip-hop producer would call "beats." Back in the days of *Soul Train*, Don Cornelius would've called it "the groove that makes you want to move real smooth." Whatever the terminology, it's that combination of drum pattern, bass line, percussion, keyboard, and guitar parts that sets up a song's tempo and gets a crowd bobbing their heads, pumping their fists, line dancing, or slam dancing. The construction of that kind of rhythm may not technically fall under the definition of "songwriting." But when it comes to crafting songs that sell, it's far too valuable a skill to ignore.

In fact, rhythm is one of the most valuable weapons in a songwriter's arsenal. You can use rhythm to revitalize your old songs with a fresh, contemporary feel. You can invent new beats that will make your song sound ground-breaking, rather than derivative. Rhythm is what you use to make that all-important first impression, infusing your song with the energy that radio pro-grammers, club DJs, video-game designers, and advertising agencies demand. If you want credibility with a contemporary audience, you have to learn to communicate with beats in the same way that you do with lyric or melody. Today, the groove is a kind of songwriter's American Express. You definitely don't want to leave home without it.

Why Rhythm Reigns

Popular music's ever-increasing emphasis on rhythm is a result of trends that extend beyond music into all realms of popular culture. Some of it stems from a simple change in demographics. As our society becomes more diverse, black and Latin American culture, both of which have musical traditions that are rooted in rhythm, increasingly influence our music.

At the same time, the information age has seen a massive increase in the sheer volume of music and other entertainment available, which has, in turn, resulted in an ever-shrinking public attention span. An aggressive rhythmic approach is perfectly suited to the modern music audience, because rhythm's impact is immediate and physical.

Rhythm Strikes First

Whenever we take a road trip, I allow my wife control over the radio, primarily to keep her distracted from my driving. To see her surf the various channels, affording each song approximately ten seconds to make its impact, is to understand the need for fast-acting entertainment. This is not a revelation to anyone in the business of radio.

In fact, it's the reason for those ten-second call-out hooks that so vex the record labels. Today's audience demands almost immediate gratification, with little patience for development or dramatic builds. If a song is going to catch the listener, it better do it fast.

For all its beauty, melody needs a little time to work its magic. After all, it takes at least eight measures to construct the whole shape of even one melodic phrase. Likewise, harmonic progressions don't happen all at once. It takes a minute to see where the chord pattern is leading. Lyrics tell a story, which can only unfold gradually. The danger is that my wife may have hit the dial before the song ever makes it to the big melodic peak or the clever lyrical twist.

Rhythm, on the other hand, is immediate. Within one or two measures, the listener can feel the basic beat of the song. Although a good arrangement may build up the rhythmic components gradually, adding a tambourine in the chorus or a conga in the second verse, the fundamental groove is established within the first few seconds and rarely drops out for more than a measure or two. As soon as you hear the first bar of Timbaland's "Give It to Me," you feel the impact of the groove. By the third measure, you're tapping your fingers on the steering wheel.

That type of physical response is the other key to rhythm's appeal. In a society where multitasking is a way of life, most people are engaged in at least one other activity while they're listening to music. Perhaps they're driving a car. Maybe they're studying for an exam. Quite possibly, they're listening to their iPods while IM-ing their friends, downloading a new ringtone, and looking at videos on their phones. In other words, don't expect a lot of intense concentration from your listeners.

One appeal of rhythm is that it doesn't require much thought. Unlike melody or lyrics, we don't contemplate rhythm—we just respond to it, largely on a physical level. Melody appeals to our intellectual sense of structure and shape, theme and variation, tension and release. Lyrics appeal to our love of language and story. Rhythm goes straight to the body. The force of it bypasses our conscious understanding and registers with us on a more subliminal level. To understand a melody or a lyric, we have to listen and think. To understand rhythm, we only have to hear and feel.

Picking Up the Pace

Given all this, it's no wonder that most radio stations favor up-tempo records over ballads. After all, it's not only songs that get tuned out by trigger-happy, ADD–afflicted audiences. It's also radio stations. Programmers are looking for songs that raise the energy level and pick up the pace, not ones that slow things down. In a time that demands immediate gratification, most MDs opt for a general approach of "harder, faster, and louder."

In fact, almost every sector of the media and entertainment world is headed in the same direction. As movies try to compete with video games, they up the level of action and demand aggressive, up-tempo music that keeps pace with what's onscreen. Advertising has moved from using songs like "Volare" in car ads, to tapping Led Zeppelin or Groove Armada for tunes, with the hopes of creating a younger, more dynamic image. Even a ballad-oriented artist like Celine Dion went with the more rhythmic "I Drove All Night" to kick off her Chrysler advertising campaign.

While some may view the emphasis on rhythm in today's music as a negative indicator of an increasingly impatient and superficial pop culture, and traditionalists might deem the ascendancy of beat makers like Timbaland or the Neptunes as the triumph of drum programmers over composers, the reality of rhythm's place in today's popular music goes deeper than just its current appeal. It's not simply that rhythm is the language of the contemporary audience. It's that rhythm is itself, by nature, contemporary.

Gimme a Beat! Gimme a New Beat!

In many ways, the story of popular music in America easily could be traced through the evolution of rhythm. From the invention of ragtime at the start of the 1900s, which first introduced African American rhythms into popular culture, the driving force in pop songwriting has been the insatiable desire for a new beat—ragtime gave way to jazz and the blues, which in turn led to swing, which evolved into rock 'n' roll. Whole eras can be defined by specific rhythms and the dances they inspired, whether it's the "jitterbugging" of the swing era, "The Twist" in the sixties, or the "Soulja Boy" for the YouTube generation. Rhythm marks the changing of time, not only in a musical sense but also in a historical one. And rhythm, like time, never stands still.

Nothing makes a pop song sound more relevant or fashionable than a hot new beat. Likewise, nothing more quickly marks a song as tired or passé than a rhythmic approach that's a year or two behind the times. "Let's Twist Again" sounded great in 1961. By 1965, it would have sounded hopelessly old-fashioned. The melodies and chord progressions might have endured, but the rhythms had been left in the dust. In the same way, a hip-hop song like "Bust a Move" by Young MC, a club classic in 1994, sounds quaint next to the hip-hop of today. Like a hard-charging train, rhythm moves relentlessly forward. A songwriter must get onboard or be passed by.

The Songwriter's Challenge

Spend an hour with the local radio station in your genre, and analyze the next eight up-tempo or mid-tempo songs that you hear.

1. Every genre will have several different types of up-tempo and mid-tempo rhythmic feels. Using a metronome, can you identify the range in tempos between the various songs? What tempos showed up most frequently?

2. Listen to the rhythmic pattern that the drums are playing. Try to single out the general pattern of the kick drum (that's the low bass drum thumping in your speakers), the snare drum (it's probably thwacking away on beats two and four), and the high hat or ride cymbal (that high percussive sound). If you can identify what each part is doing, then you can begin to recognize the rhythmic feel. Can you hear the basic repetitive pattern? Do you hear that same pattern recurring in several different songs?

3. Especially in certain rock styles, much of the beat depends on the way the arrangement develops. Listen for the way the drums change from section to section. Are there large dynamic or rhythmic shifts in the song? How does the rhythm develop through the course of the song?

4. Once you've identified one or two recurring rhythms, try putting them into action. If you have a Pro Tools system or a drum machine, you can program the patterns and try to play along. See if you can write a new song to those rhythms, or try out an old song with the new grooves.

5. If you don't have any means to record the rhythm patterns, lock the feel in your head by playing along with records

that have a similar groove. Keeping that
new contemporary feel, try playing your
own song. Can you sense your music
moving a little closer to fitting a radio
format?

Bring That Beat Back

At the same time that popular beats go in or out of style, other older rhythms are being recycled and renewed. Sooner or later, everything that's old becomes new again. The blues shuffle rhythm of Lightnin' Hopkins and T-Bone Walker, popularized in the forties, shows up underneath early rock 'n' roll hits like "Kansas City" in the fifties, returns in songs like "Midnight Rambler" in the sixties, then shows up as the basis of seventies rock anthems like "Walk This Way" and "Can't Get Enough." The swing feel of classic jazz was reinvented by urban producer Teddy Riley in the eighties, filtered through the modern technology of drum machines, and turned into "new jack" hits like "Groove Me" and "Just Got Paid." Today, it's been recycled yet again by Christina Aguilera, with "Candyman." Using the classic "Bo Diddley" rhythm of the fifties, George Michael donned a black leather jacket and had a hit with "Faith" almost two decades after that groove was first popularized.

Indeed, because specific rhythms are so identified with the particular era that created them, a recycled rhythm can immediately recall another time and place. Early punk-rockers like the Ramones adapted their trademark drum pattern to allude to the early fifties. Now, modern rockers adapt the same groove to allude to the Ramones. Prince harkened back to James Brown by adapting his grooves.

> If you want to summon up the spirit of another period, the quickest way to do it is not through melody or chords but through rhythm.

The Songwriter's Challenge

Let's go back in time. Choose a favorite historical period from the last hundred years, and do some musical research. What was the popular rhythm and dance of the day? If you're back in the twenties, you'll find Dixieland and the Charleston. If you're in the seventies, think disco and "the hustle."

After listening to enough music to put the older groove securely in your head, see if you can adapt one of your songs to that classic rhythm pattern. You'll need to experiment, as mixing and matching tempos or rhythms can be tricky. But when it works, you'll find a new old beat that instantly sets your song apart.

Dancing to a Different Drum

In the same way that a new song can resurrect an old rhythm, a new or unexpected beat can often reinvigorate a musical style or artist on the verge of stagnation. Think of how Dido separated herself from the pack of female singer-songwriters through the chilled-out, clubby beats of her brother, Rollo Armstrong. By using a more aggressive, rock-oriented rhythm approach, country acts like Rascal Flatts and Garth Brooks opened the genre to a new, younger audience. Whether it's the Bee Gees adapting to the disco craze of the seventies or Nelly Furtado and Gwen Stefani embracing hip-hop beats today, savvy artists know that the key to reinvention usually lies in rhythm. By and large, beats are what make a song or an artist contemporary.

The Songwriter's Challenge

For this one, you'll need to think like a remixer. In fact, if you have the recording tools, try recording or sampling a beat to use as the basis of this experiment. For those without the means to record, think about purchasing one of the hundreds of sample "drum loop" CDs or downloads available through companies like Modernbeats.com or Beta Monkey. It doesn't have to cost money. On sites like Looperman.com, you can choose from hundreds of drum loops and play along with the beat of your choice.

The art lies in choosing the right rhythm. Look for a beat well outside of your own style but with a tempo that will match up comfortably with one of your songs. If your genre is hip-hop, try out a rock groove. If you write country, mix it with a swing or Latin feel. Play your song along with the different rhythm and see if the sparks fly. As with DNA's remix of "Tom's Diner," it's the unexpected chemistry of different musical elements thrown together that can create something surprising and new.

We know from our own listening experience that a fresh beat can make an old song or style feel more current. But what makes the beat itself contemporary? Why does one rhythmic approach feel fresh and exciting, while another feels like it's dragging the song down? After all, in the world of popular music, almost every song will be in 4/4 time. Almost every drum pattern will include a snare or clap on beats two and four. Almost every rhythmic feel will either be based on a subdivision of sixteenth notes or eighth notes. That doesn't leave all that much room for variation. And yet, hip-hop producers, dance remixers, rock drummers, and reggae "riddim" programmers constantly discover new ways to make their rhythms innovative and compelling. The key lies in understanding that there is more to rhythm than a drum pattern and more to energy than just tempo.

Sound and Fury
Signify Everything

It's not too surprising that most of the rock era's rhythmically inventive songwriters were also record producers, from Leiber & Stoller, James Brown, and Stevie Wonder, right up until today, with Rodney Jerkins and J.R. Rotem. Rhythm and sound are inextricably linked, and the creation of a new beat requires sensitivity to both elements.

It's not merely a matter of what musical parts are being played. What counts most is how the drums, bass, and percussion sound when they're playing the parts. The trademark "boom, boom, thwack" of "We Will Rock You" would be an entirely different beat if it were played on a conga and cowbell. The actual drum pattern of a seventies disco classic like "Ain't No Stoppin' Us Now" and a techno-house hit like "Pump Up the Jam" have very little that differentiates them. But because the former is built on the sound of a live drummer and bass player, and the latter is the obviously electronic sound of a Roland 707, they register as two entirely different rhythm patterns.

Putting on the Producer Hat

For many songwriters, the greatest challenge in creating new and innovative rhythms lies in accepting that it's their job to do so at all. "Isn't that what producers are for?" they ask. Yes, of course it is. However, the music industry issued a memo several years ago that many songwriters seem to have missed:

ATTENTION: CHANGE IN JOB DESCRIPTION.
Songwriters are now producers as well.

Unless you're the kind of topline writer who adds melody and lyrics to already-assembled tracks (in which case your challenge will be to find the best producers and the hottest beats), you are now responsible not only for the substance of your song but also for how it sounds to the A&R people, managers, artists, and audiences that are hearing it. Changes in musical styles, the amazing advances in home recording technology, and the dearth of experienced, imaginative A&R people have conspired to eliminate the distinction between a song and a "record." This doesn't mean that you must have the ability to do all the arranging, engineering, and mixing on your own (although many successful songwriters do). It does mean that all of those aspects of production are now officially your problem to solve, because your song will be judged in part by the quality of the *entire* product.

As a producer, you're not only responsible for how your song sounds but how it feels. One of the primary concerns of any experienced producer is ensuring that a song's groove is unique, fitting, and sufficiently exciting to get a crowd moving. This means taking into account the overall sonic quality of the rhythm track and how each instrument or part fits into the groove. Is the kick drum big and earthshaking or small and pointed? Is the snare drum exaggerated and aggressive, like in Janet Jackson's "Nasty," or natural sounding and funky, like in Jamiroquai's "Virtual Insanity"? Do the percussion parts feel live and loose or tightly programmed and computer corrected? All of these factors, along with the use of reverbs, compression, and other effects, define the rhythm and determine how effective the beat will be. Imagine a beat like Kanye West's "Stronger" without the reverb-heavy, industrial quality of the snare sound. It would be another rhythm entirely.

The Machine with a Thousand Moving Parts

As important as each individual sound can be in shaping a rhythmic feel, the job of creating a groove doesn't end with discovering an earthshaking kick drum or a woofer-blowing bass sound. Aspiring beat makers must also consider how all the various elements in the track sound together. Rhythm is a cumulative effect, a product of the interaction between each musical element in the song. A funky drumbeat alone will not fill a dance floor. Rather, it's how the drumbeat fits with the bass line, and the guitar part, and ultimately the vocal melody that determines whether a particular groove is effective.

The Jackson Five's "ABC" is a classic groove not because of one specific part but as a result of the perfect interplay between the bass line, the distorted guitar riff, the drums, and the piano part. Rhythm requires a songwriter not only to think like a producer or engineer but also like an arranger. You need to consider the natural movement of the melody and the chord progression within a particular song, identify the parts of the rhythm that need to be accented, and then create other parts that will complement the basic groove. It requires a coordinated effort, with all the elements of a production working together, to create a rhythm with an unstoppable forward momentum.

That kind of momentum, much more than the actual number of beats per minute, is what distinguishes a song as "up-tempo." Dance songs tend to be 120 bpm and above; punk-pop songs could be much faster; hip-hop songs will often be considerably slower, clocking in somewhere around 90 bpm. Nevertheless, a song from each genre might register as equally "up-tempo" to a group of casual listeners.

A song's energy level is a product of the groove and the aggressiveness with which it's played, not the actual tempo.

What really qualifies a song as up-tempo is the level of aggressiveness and the compelling forward momentum of the song's groove. "Can I Get A..." by Jay-Z is almost half the tempo of "American Idiot" by Green Day, but to a casual listener they will both register as up-tempo songs. Conversely, a song like "Good Riddance (Time of Your Life)" is actually faster than the Jay-Z song but feels more like a ballad, because of the laid-back nature of the arrangement.

The Songwriter's Challenge

No effective rhythm track comes together without plenty of trial and error and a willingness to acknowledge when the groove just doesn't feel right. Choose one of your songs, and let's walk through the process:

1. Is there a rhythmic pattern built into the song's melody or harmonic progression that the track needs to emphasize? Or is it more effective for the bass and drums to contrast with the rhythm of the lead vocal line? Listen to Whitney Houston's "How Will I Know" and notice how the bassline and keyboard emphasize the rhythm of the hook in the chorus, but then contrast with the vocal in the verses.

2. Is there a key instrumental part around which you can build the rest of the groove? Think of the guitar part in Natalie Imbruglia's "Torn."

3. Once the foundation of the groove is in place, is there an instrument that could play counter to the rhythm, to add interest? Check out what the guitar is doing in Maroon Five's "This Love."

4. How is everything working together? Does the groove feel like it's constantly pushing ahead or holding back? Does the tempo feel slow? Does the momentum sustain, even in sections with no vocal?

If you feel the need to repeatedly raise the tempo, your rhythm arrangement is probably dragging things down. It may be a matter of improving the drum and bass patterns or finding a guitar or keyboard part that will keep things grooving, rather than just picking up the pace.

Running the Rhythm Game
Midi Mafia
SONGWRITERS

Without question, nothing has elevated the importance of rhythm in pop music more than the rise of hip-hop and the dominant role that urban music now plays in pop culture. When Nelly duets with Tim McGraw and tops the country charts, it's clear that rap music and hip-hop have transcended their roots in black culture and now influence popular music on every level. Behind this spreading influence are not only the artists themselves but also multitudes of young producers and writers whose spirit of experimentation, independence, and entrepreneurial street-savvy is a perfect throwback to classic hit makers like Phil Spector, Berry Gordy, and Gamble & Huff.

With hits like "21 Questions" for 50 Cent and "When I See You" for Fantasia, Midi Mafia is one of the hottest of these young production teams. Representing the combined talents of rapper Bruce Waynne and turntablist/engineer Dirty Swift, Midi Mafia has evolved from beat makers to hit songwriters, with an approach that combines raw, youthful energy with a wide-ranging knowledge of music history. Their comments give a behind-the-scenes glimpse into the working methods of contemporary urban writer-producers and a sense of the attention to detail required of those who want to create hit records.

SWIFT: With "When I See You," we were in the studio collaborating with the Mzmeriq guys (Sam Watters and Louis Biancaniello). We work a lot with people from different genres, because sometimes it brings something extra to the table. I was coming up with a track and some drums, and we were all sitting around playing with melodies. We just wanted to keep it real minimal. The static part of the record was the real hook of the beat. There's a lot of record noise in there, because we wanted it to be pretty, but with some real grime in the drums. When I mixed it, I wanted the record to feel real young and tight and punchy.

That's also why I try to mix as much of our stuff as possible. I like to be there from the beginning to end. If I had the time, I'd be at the mastering session— it's that important to us. There's nothing worse than doing a hot record in the studio, then not being involved in the mix, and hearing it come out all messed up. You might get an engineer that says, "Oh this sounds terrible, let me clean this up, get the static out of there."

BRUCE: When you're first getting in the game, you're not quite sure what to do. Then you realize that no one knows what they're doing, and so you might as well do things yourself. That demo mix of the Fantasia record was the one Clive Davis loved. He didn't want to change anything.

Just as the success of "When I See You" repositioned Fantasia for a youth-driven market, the rhythmic energy and lyrical attitude of hip-hop is being sought by acts across the musical spectrum, to capture a generation raised on beats and rhymes. For urban-based writers like Midi Mafia, that just means more opportunity to expand their game into new musical markets, draw on new sources of inspiration, and stay one step ahead of everyone else.

SWIFT: Let's face it: The majority of the Hot 100 is urban stuff. It's what the young kids listen to, so if you want to be in the game, you have to use it. If you're a rock artist who wants to stretch your wings, you want to go with what the kids are listening to. Personally, I think it would be cool to get with some country writers, and see what they would do on some hip-hop tracks. Who's more hip-hop than Johnny Cash? He basically rapped a lot of his songs; he dressed all in black.

BRUCE: Hip-hop is a culture that's transcended colors and ethnicity. It's really a vibe. Hip-hop is clothes, it's the way you talk, it's the way you dress, the swagger, the style. The music is how we push all of it. When you get someone like Justin Timberlake, he's the underdog. He's a white kid coming out of the pop-est group ever, but he loves R&B and soul music. He's the underdog—and hip-hop has always been about the underdog. Rap started as a black thing, but it's not a black thing anymore. Now, it's all about the vibe. If you got it, you got it.

SWIFT: Me and Bruce, we listen to a lot of different music. Sometimes it's the old Stax stuff. Or, if I'm driving the car, it might be classic rock stations. You can't really listen strictly to the genre you're in; you have to listen to a little bit of everything. Hip-hop really started from breakbeats, and older, different genres of music, so you have to kind of keep going there. You never know where you're going to find a melody or maybe something to sample or a drum idea.

BRUCE: You gotta do your homework.

SWIFT: We also have other producers who are coming up under us, who we're helping out. They have the time to go digging through vinyl, so they'll be putting us onto new things. We have one guy who's into going over to Japan and getting records over there. He's digging and finding different sounds, chopping them up. Ideas can come from anywhere, really.

BRUCE: We just make sure to stay ahead of the game. We'll do things where people are like, "I don't

know. This is too much…" Then later they'll be like—
"Oh yeah, man, we should have done that before. We
should have listened to you guys." We just let people
follow our lead.

SWIFT: That's why we don't really chase the
sound of the day or the trends or whatever keyboard
everyone is using at the moment. We're conscious of
it—you have to be aware of what's going on in the
business. But I think a hit record is a hit record no
matter what. We're still selling beats we did three
years ago. You can dress it up a bit to make it lean one
way or the other, depending on what the climate is,
but a hit record is always going to win.

Writing the Rhythm

Particularly for those with a more traditional music background,
the dominant role that rhythm now plays in popular music can be
a source of frustration and resentment, as if the rules of the songwriting game have somehow been changed to accommodate a new
set of players. And yet, we've seen that the principles of hit songwriting apply as much to rhythm as they do to melody or lyrics.
Beats must make an impact and establish an identity for the song in
the same way that a lyrical concept does. A rhythm pattern needs a
balance of predictability and surprise, no less than any good

melody does. Just as the sound of the words will determine how well a lyric "sings," the sound of the drums and bass will affect how well the rhythm communicates.

Most important, the power of a groove depends on all of the various rhythmic components coming together in ways both complementary and contrasting, which is exactly how lyrics, melody, chord progression, and, yes, rhythm, combine to create a whole song. The ascendance of rhythm does not detract from the other aspects of songwriting but supports them and keeps them relevant to an increasingly distracted audience. Without a rhythm track's ability to grab listeners immediately on a physical level, the clever lyric twist or brilliant chord change might never be heard. As strong as your chorus might be, it still needs the momentum of a groove to carry it along.

When it comes to the ingredients that make a hit, a good title, a memorable melody, and a hot rhythm track are enough to get you started. But it's not until you mix all of those things together that you come up with the most important ingredient of all—the one thing no hit can do without. Rhythm can set the stage, but where rhythm meets melody meets lyrical concept, that's where you'll find your hook.

CHAPTER ELEVEN

Hits Need Hooks
To Keep Us Hanging On

Everyone knows about hooks. In fact, the one thing that every songwriter, singer, A&R person, manager, radio promoter, or casual music fan seems to be certain of is that you need a good hook. This much is true. As I discussed as far back as chapter two, a hook is simply the thing that makes a song memorable. It's hard to have a hit if no one remembers the song.

Although most writers will assure you that their song has a great hook, they often can't identify exactly where that hook is or why it's memorable. Some writers think hooks and choruses are synonymous, but they're not. A chorus is usually at least eight measures long, which is far too extended for a hook. Some writers assume that the hook is the title. It may be. Often, though, titles are too short to be a hook all by themselves. Granted, just because you can't precisely locate your hook doesn't mean that it isn't there. Still, it might mean that the hook is too subtle to catch most casual listeners.

I hate to break it to you after you've ventured this far into the book, but neither I nor anyone else can tell you how to write a great hook. The ability to create memorable hooks stems only partly from knowledge. It also relies on inspiration, natural talent, and pure dumb luck, which is why even the greatest songwriters in history could only do it occasionally.

What this chapter can do is to help you recognize what a hook is, show you where it should be placed in the song, and outline what it should do to be memorable. On top of that, it can let you in on the secret that separates the top professional songwriters from the many aspiring writers around them:

There's more than one kind of hook.

There are HOOKS, and hooks, and then there are hooks. When it comes to making a song memorable, it often takes all three types to do the job.

The Primary Hook

If you're trying to catch a big fish, you need a big hook to do it. Naturally, a hit song is one that appeals to a large audience, so it makes sense that most hit songs have a big, fat, juicy hook to pull in the masses. While some songs subtly sneak in and exert their hold through a cool vibe or a great performance, most hits place their hooks front, center, and shining for all the world to see. A good primary hook should be easy to spot.

Do you remember the ten-second call-out sample that's used by radio to test a record? For all practical purposes, this is the definition of a primary hook. After all, if you can't find a ten-second excerpt of your song that captures a listener, then on a very fundamental level, you don't have the hook you need to get the song on the radio. If you can't get it on the radio, then the song is not a single.

We can safely say that a primary hook is roughly three to five measures long, depending on the tempo of the song. That's longer than the title, although it likely includes the title. It's well short of a full chorus. To go back to good ol' "My Girl," it's:

"My girl
Talkin' 'bout my girl…
My girl."

That's about ten seconds. And that's a hook.

Four Characteristics of a Primary Hook

The brief lyric you read above is hardly the only memorable part of "My Girl." Like many classic Motown songs, "My Girl" has big hooks, little hooks, hidden hooks, and hooks that have yet to be defined. If one hook doesn't catch you, another one will. Nevertheless, if you had to explain to a wedding band from outer space how "My Girl" goes, that's probably the hook you'd use. That excerpt has all four characteristics of a primary hook:

A PRIMARY HOOK IS A PEAK MOMENT While the melody actually moves down for the first line of the hook in "My Girl," it subsequently leaps up for the final payoff, that last repeat of the song's title. After the B-section has raised the tension on every level, the chorus arrives to deliver the emotional resolution. All of the lyrical questions have been resolved (How does one have sunshine on a cloudy day?), and the melodic build has reached its apex.

Old-school songwriting wisdom suggests that if you want your hook to stand out, you should match the title phrase with the highest notes of the melody. On a purely physical level, the notes that are highest in register will get the most emphasis from the singer, which all but guarantees an emotional climax at that particular point. Naturally, then, those high notes are not a bad place to put your hook. It's a technique that's been used on everything from "Do You Wanna Dance?" to "Take It to the Limit." You can't argue with success.

A PRIMARY HOOK IS PROMINENT Again, those old Motown and Brill Building writers knew what they were doing. Songs like "He's So Fine" don't waste any time getting to the hook—they place it in the very first line of the song. "Stop! In the Name of Love" is a classic hook, with the title set to the peak notes in the melody and placed unmistakably in the first line of the chorus. Adhering to country form, "You'll Think of Me" puts the hook at the end of each four-bar phrase, so it appears in the middle and as the last line of the chorus. There is a natural prominence to the first and last line of any section in a song. If you want something to be remembered, this is where you put it.

Keep in mind, though: The hook and the title are not necessarily the same thing. In "You'll Think of Me," the real hook is the opening phrase of the chorus. The title itself is a poignant response to the actual hook. In another typical hook construction, the hook begins with a setup line and then follows with the title: "I'm going down, down, down/In a burning ring of fire." Sometimes it takes two phrases to create the whole hook.

If your hook is out of position, buried somewhere in a verse or stuck in an awkward spot in the chorus, you may need to reinforce it. Perhaps you can use it to set up the whole song, by letting it stand alone at the beginning of the introduction. Alternatively, you can try creating a "tag" section—a four- or eight-bar interlude after each chorus, in which the hook can be brought back and repeated. Nothing helps a hook like repetition.

A PRIMARY HOOK BEARS REPEATING Didn't I just say that? Like it or not, the lines in a song that you choose to repeat will register as the hook. In the same way, no matter how strong you think your hook is, without repetition, few listeners will find it. Repetition cues the audience that a particular part of the song is important. Whether the hook is memorable depends on the quality of what's being repeated.

To create a hook that's memorable, rather than merely repetitive, you need a melodic or lyrical idea that makes an impact all by itself, independent of the lines around it. "No, we're never gonna survive, unless we get a little crazy" is an idea that stands alone—it's interesting enough to sustain repetition. Another phrase from the verse of the same song might be effective in advancing the story, but it can't stand alone. Nor does it bear repeating.

A banal or vague hook will be hurt by repetition, rather than helped.

As listeners, we're not required to remember anything that's repeated. A hook must deserve repetition. That means it must offer the listener something more than what he or she expected.

A PRIMARY HOOK PACKS A PUNCH Whether it's a melodic twist or a lyrical one, an unexpected chord change, or a drastic change in the rhythm, the unexpected is by nature more memorable than the same old, same old. Rihanna's hit "Unfaithful" felt like a typical "I used to love him, but now I don't" ballad, until the last line of the chorus, "I don't wanna be...a murderer."

Wow. What did she just say? No one expects the word *murderer* to show up in a pop ballad, so the shock element creates an instant hook. Wherever the big twist in your song is, there your hook will be also.

The Songwriter's Challenge

Whether it's an unexpected melodic turn, a play on words, or a clever lyrical payoff of the verse that came before, try to identify the twist in your own song.

Is it the title line? Is it contained within the ten-second call-out hook? Is it in the chorus at all? Does it appear more than once in the song?

If your twist is getting lost, then you're not treating it like a hook. Try to:

1. Restructure the song to make the twist either the first or last line of the chorus.

2. Retitle the song, to make your lyrical twist the song's calling card.

3. Add a "tag" section to reinforce your key line, or reprise that line at the beginning or end of the song.

4. Echo the melodic twist in an instrumental part somewhere in the arrangement.

You shouldn't have to search long to find your song's primary hook. Indeed, given the nature of the ten-second call-out sample, you won't be given long to hit the listener with what is presumably your best shot. But the primary hook is not your only shot. There's much more to a song than that, and hopefully more in the way of hooks as well. As we've already started to see, a song needs not only one big hook, but a lot of smaller ones as well.

The Secondary Hook

A secondary hook shares all of the same basic characteristics of a primary hook. It maintains a position of prominence, often as the featured element in the introduction, in an interlude, or in the final chorus of the song. While a secondary hook doesn't have to repeat, it usually does, sometimes more than the primary hook. Like any good musical or lyrical idea, a secondary hook will also carry an element of surprise.

However, a secondary hook is not *the* surprise. It is not the central twist to the song. In Dire Straits' "Money for Nothing," the refrain of "I want my MTV" is an unforgettable, definitive element. Yet as powerful as that line is, it doesn't replace the primary hook, which is the title line. Instead, the secondary hook adds to the central primary hook, which is precisely what it's supposed to do.

The secondary hook is like a great supporting actor. Rather than steal the scene, it only makes the star and the story that much better. A secondary hook doesn't compete with the central twist, nor does it occur at the emotional peak of the song. There is only room for one hook in those all-important moments, and that turf belongs to the primary hook. Secondary hooks show up in the other spots within the song to reinforce the primary hook or to offer some kind of contrast.

A secondary hook should not be less effective than the primary hook. No song needs that. In fact, one danger of secondary hooks is that a weak one can distract from the primary hook and lessen, rather than intensify, the song's impact. In the same way, no amount of clever and catchy secondary hooks can compensate for a flimsy primary hook. They are, by nature, two different things.

Going Back for Seconds

I've said it before: One of the most significant differences between aspiring songwriters and seasoned hit makers is the use of secondary hooks. Even novice songwriters recognize the need for a primary hook. Experienced writers know that one hook is not enough, and they search out opportunities to add secondary hooks. Some of these are built directly into the song form, such as an interlude after the chorus, a recurring line in the verse ("Hey There Delilah"), or a variation on the chorus during the final fade. Other secondary hooks are instrumental parts that fit behind the vocal line, introducing new melodic themes that work in counterpoint to the primary melody.

In their own way, secondary hooks can often be as prominent as primary hooks. The "free, free/set them free" refrain of "If You Love Somebody Set Them Free" is really a second chorus. Can you imagine "Just the Way You Are" without the sax melody? The piano voicings in "Lean on Me" make that chord progression an instantly recognizable secondary hook; the guitar part in Tom Petty's "Free Falling" does the same for that song. Some secondary hooks reinforce the primary hook, like the "think it over" line that follows "Stop! In the Name of Love." Others offer a contrasting element, like the "La, la" part in "Crocodile Rock."

There's always room for a second hook.

No matter how they're used, all secondary hooks fill the same function: to keep pulling the listeners in, even while giving them a rest from the primary hook.

The Songwriter's Challenge

If your song is missing a supporting hook, you can spur your imagination by taking a look at the primary one. The trick is to find something that will reinforce the main premise of the song, by doing what your primary hook doesn't.

1. If your lyrical hook appears only once in the chorus, you need a secondary hook that repeats that lyrical phrase in a different melodic or harmonic setting.

2. If you have a title that repeats frequently, build your secondary hook on a new idea, a response to the primary hook.

3. When your chorus is active melodically or rhythmically busy, try for a second hook that's more spacious and relaxed.

4. If your lyric is a very intricate story, then let your secondary hook be melodic or rhythmic, with no lyric at all.

Keep in mind though that a secondary hook should offer a brief diversion, not an endless distraction. The challenge of secondary hooks is to avoid the law of diminishing returns mentioned earlier. If ten different elements in the song are trying to be memorable, none will be. Somehow, you have to keep the audience engaged but avoid overwhelming them with one catchy idea after another. This doesn't necessarily mean that you reduce the number of hooks. It just means that you learn how to hide some of them.

The Hidden Hook

When I was young and first began to play guitar, I would often buy the sheet music of my favorite song. There in front of me, I would find the melody, the lyric, the chords, the tablature, and a rudimentary piano arrangement. Even with my limited skills, I was quickly able to strum along and pluck out something that resembled the song. Yet something was always missing. No matter how hard I studied the pages in front of me, a part of the song that I considered essential was nowhere to be found. The sheet music was missing the hidden hooks.

They were invisible because hidden hooks are not part of the song. In fact, we could expand the traditional definition of a song to include not just melody and lyrics but chord progression as well, and the hidden hooks still would not be included. Hidden hooks are production and arranging elements, and therefore they fall outside the precise job description of a songwriter. Nevertheless, they often emerge as the most identifiable parts of a hit record. That killer bass line, the talkbox effect, the opening drum fill, or that part where the whole record just stops, then starts up again—trust me, you won't find it in the sheet music.

So why does it belong in a book about songwriting? It goes right back to that changing job description I discussed in the previous chapter.

Songwriting is no longer only about songwriting.

Like beats, bass lines, and drum sounds, hidden hooks are relevant because they are part of your new toolbox as a songwriter-producer. Sheet music is no longer an accurate representation of the songwriter's craft. There's more to hit making than meets the eye.

The good news is that although they may be "hidden" in the production, these hooks are not hard to identify. They may be core musical elements, like the bass line in Michael Jackson's "Billie Jean" or the guitar part in "Dirty Diana." It could be the shuffle feel of "The Way You Make Me Feel" or the swing of "Remember the Time." Sometimes, hidden hooks are sonic elements, like the snare sound on "Smooth Criminal" or the delay effects on the vocal of "Human Nature." Sometimes, they're shameless gimmicks, like the Vincent Price spoken bit in "Thriller." Whether it's clever recording engineering or great arranging, if it's sufficiently memorable, it qualifies as a hidden hook. If it works, use it.

Of course, great performers add their own hooks as well. Whether it's the teary ending to "She's Out of My Life" or the "just look over your shoulders, honey...ooh" ad lib on "I'll Be There," there's a reason that Michael Jackson is/was the King of Pop. His gift for nuance has been apparent since he was seven years old, even in the earliest vocals. In the same way, he and producers like Quincy Jones were able to pinpoint the musicians who would add hooks of their own, like Eddie Van Halen and the "Beat It" guitar solo. Those moments may not be part of the song itself, but they are certainly part of what made those songs memorable.

Honing Those Hidden Hooks

It's easy to recognize the value of a brilliant production touch or an inspired vocal performance. To incorporate those elements into your songwriting skill set is a much taller order. Am I recommending that you create a hit song by having Michael Jackson sing it and Eddie Van Halen play the guitar solo? You could get worse advice. What I'm suggesting is that a songwriter can no longer afford to leave those kinds of defining moments solely up to the record "producer" or the artist. Even if you're not the next Quincy Jones, here are four tips for "writing" the hidden hooks.

BANISH THE WORD "DEMO" FROM YOUR VOCABULARY You'll be about the last person to do it. The idea of a "demo"—a rough, unpolished recording of the song used to "demonstrate" the song to artists—continues to exist solely in the minds of songwriters. Artists, A&R people, and others who listen to these demos quit using the term years ago. As far as these decision makers are concerned, when they're listening to music, they're playing a "record." If you feel a song needs a big snare sound or a string section to make it into a hit, then that's what you need to play for them. Given the availability of home recording technology, no excuses are accepted.

MAKE EVERY LINE A MELODY AND EVERY PART A HOOK Apply your basic hook-writing principles to your hidden hooks. A great bass line or guitar solo is no different than a great melody line. It should feature a certain amount of repetition, as well as a clever, unexpected twist. Treat every part in the production as if it were a primary hook or secondary hook, and you'll usually wind up creating some good hidden hooks in the process.

THINK LIKE A COMPOSER, NOT A SONGWRITER Too many songwriters take the lazy way out. By drawing a distinction between the arrangement, the production, and the song itself, they reduce the song to nothing but its most basic elements. Imagine if Beethoven took that approach on the Fifth Symphony: "Well, it just goes, buh, buh, buh, BUHM. And then it sort of repeats."

Picture your song as a symphony. The bass line, percussion parts, string lines, and the guitar riffs are all part of the whole composition. The peaks and valleys of the arrangement are as much a part of the song as the plotline of the lyric. If that sounds difficult to pull off—it is. Read the biographies of Phil Spector or Brian Wilson. Hit making was never a walk in the park.

The Songwriter's Challenge

It's time to make your masterpiece. Take one of your own choruses and try to go further than you've ever gone in dreaming up the entire scope of the arrangement and production. Imagine what instruments you'll need to realize the sound in your head. Define specifically what part each instrument will play. Envision the sonic character of the recording: Will it be big and bombastic or warm and intimate?

Nothing is outside your control, and no detail is too small.

If it all feels a little overwhelming, here are three basic arranging and production principles to guide you:

1. Fill the spaces.

The basis of all arranging is counterpoint. This just means that when one line (a vocal melody, for instance) is moving, other melodic lines rest (or play longer, sustained notes). When the principal melody rests, then the other lines become more active and fill in the gaps. Think of a Bach Invention, or the Earth, Wind, and Fire horn section.

2. Find a model.

Try to identify an already existing production that has something close to the sound you're seeking. Notice all of the details that are making that record work, and adapt them to your own song. Even Phil Spector copied Berry Gordy, and vice versa.

3. Easy does it.

Don't try to add too many musical parts all at once. Let the arrangement build gradually, by introducing one or two new elements in every section. Add one instrumental part to the second verse that wasn't in the first. It's the expectation of a new surprise around every corner that keeps the listener involved.

LET ACCIDENTS HAPPEN   Lazy songwriters are one problem; control freaks are another. Vocalists are tortured until they get the melody exactly like it sounded in the writer's head. Technical problems in the studio are treated like obstacles to be overcome. There's a place for perfection, but there's also a value in keeping an open ear. Sometimes those mistakes are the moments when something utterly uncontrived and magical happens.

Danny Poku, the co-manager of Stargate Productions and one of dance music's legendary remixers (back when he was "Dancin' Danny D"), had one of his biggest records with a remix of Chaka Khan's "I'm Every Woman." During the recording of that record, wires got crossed and a snare drum fill was suddenly given a pitch bend by one of the keyboard parts. When they heard the sound, the whole roomful of musicians stopped in their tracks. Everyone then spent the next hour trying to figure out how they had achieved the effect. That drum fill effect became one of the most-used gimmicks in dance music for the next ten years. Accidents happen. Be grateful.

THE INSIDE TRACK

Little Things That Make the Big Hooks
Stargate
SONGWRITERS

For Mikkel and Tor from Stargate, fortuitous accidents are part of the relentless search for the unique moments that can define a record.

TOR: Part of the art is to let the accidents happen. It's very easy to say, "No, it's got to be like this." You have to step back a little bit and see if there's something that you can build on. Otherwise, every song we did would be predictable. We want to create something a little bit different than what we did yesterday. And we want the character of the artist or topline writer to shine through. We might be sitting there with a genius. What if you heard the early Bob Dylan demos or the early Ray Charles—would you recognize the genius in that or just run straight over it? We keep our ears open all the time for those accidents or those little unique moments, whether it's on the keyboard, or in the arrangement, or with the other writers.

Sometimes it only takes one note different in the melody to make something a hit. Let's say you have something very predictable—there's nothing wrong with it, but there's nothing special about it. Then you come up with one little change in the melody, and that's all it took.

MIKKEL: Other times, we'll scrap all the music, down to just the vocals. Then we come again and try different chords. We did something like that with "Sexy Love."

TOR: On "Sexy Love," we had a melody in the track, and Ne-Yo listened to it and changed one note. It made a world of difference. It's the difference between something that's boring and predictable and something that's special and recognizable. When he did that, we decided to change the music after his melody. We put that theme up front, and suddenly we had something unique. It's about looking for those tiny little moments that create the magic.

MIKKEL: You need something that stands out—that people will pick up on.

TOR: In "Irreplaceable," the "to the left" part was just a line in the first verse. Then, as we listened to the intro, we thought it was a little bit empty. So we said, "Let's see if we can take this 'to the left' piece and put it up front and just cut it out a couple of times." Then Beyonce picked up on it—she put it into the breakdown after the bridge and then built it up. That became the catch phrase of the whole song.

I hate to admit it, but it's the same thing that Max Martin did on "...Baby One More Time," with "Oh baby, baby." Again, it's searching for that unique statement. You have to search for those little things in the song.

For all of their willingness to experiment and to accept the occasional accident, Mikkel and Tor also recognize the need for discipline and decision making when it comes to primary hooks, secondary hooks, and hidden hooks. Going back to Tor's analogy about painter Edvard Munch and the need to draw a strongly defined line, Stargate always tries to focus their tracks on one or two defining ideas.

MIKKEL: Even though our tracks are sparse, when we're creating, we'll throw stuff on without thinking too much about it. We'll just play stuff that we're feeling with different sounds. Then later, we'll go back and select two parts, and scrap all the others, searching for that magic combination.

But once you find the right combination, you have to believe in what you have. You don't need ten sounds on your track. You need one good one—and maybe a simple beat and a few other sprinkles. But you have to believe in the core that you have.

TOR: This is the difference between a record that sounds good and a hit record. I think most hit records have that one big idea. So you have to resist the temptation of adding stuff on and just stick to that one big idea. If you don't have that big idea, then you probably don't have a hit record.

Big Hooks Pull It All Together

It's ironic that it would be the producer, the person so often immersed in the detail work of record making, who sees most clearly the importance of the "big idea." Even with all of the studio know-how, access to the best musicians and singers, and a bagful of arranging techniques and engineering tricks, Stargate and others know the cold, hard truth: No one can mask the absence of a primary hook. A hidden hook won't save a song without a central concept or a memorable melodic twist. To paraphrase a famous adage of Quincy Jones, there are some things that simply can't be shined up.

At the same time, when the primary hook is working well, all of the other pieces seem to fall into place naturally. A strong melody often suggests the right counter-line, just as a good chord progression inspires a bass pattern. A defining lyrical concept can provoke a production element that becomes a hidden hook, like the cash-register percussion part in Pink Floyd's "Money." This is one reason why songwriters so often claim that their biggest hits seemed to "write themselves." One big idea can be the catalyst for all of the small ideas, musical, lyrical, and production-related, that are necessary to construct a hit record.

> A hook is not one more element of a song, like melody or rhythm. A hook is where all of the elements come together to create something memorable.

For songwriters with little knowledge of their craft, the occasional convergence of melody, rhythm, title, and concept into one big idea is not much different than the luck of a weekend golfer who happens to hit a hole in one. It's exciting, all right, but it won't get an amateur into the PGA. A career is built on consistent performance, and that requires an understanding of the nuances of the process and a dedication to getting the details right, day in and day out.

That's why I can't end this book with a discussion of hooks. As essential as they may be, the songwriting game doesn't stop there. A hook might make a hit song, but it won't make you a hit song-writer. For that, there's still some important work left to be done.

CHAPTER TWELVE

The Finishing Touch
Let's Go All the Way

Have you ever seen a carpenter inspect another carpenter's handiwork? Have you watched a tailor look over a garment someone else has made? It's never the big things that get noticed. Instead, the experts perceive and judge the tiniest details: the way the underside of a box is finished or a button is attached. Every craftsperson knows that the mark of an expert is in the finishing touch.

So it is among professional songwriters. Anyone might come up with a primary hook that grabs an audience. It's not enough. The best songwriters don't stop with one clever, catchy idea. They follow through the process, making sure that all the details are in place and that every element in the song, every transition from section to section, every intro and every fade are the best they can be. Any lucky person in the jungle might find a diamond in the rough. The art lies in knowing how to cut and polish.

For better or worse, people buy sparkle. As I said in the previous chapter, much of songwriting's finishing work belongs more to the craft of record production than to songwriting. Nevertheless, it's these production touches that add polish to a song, until it shines and starts to sound like a hit. That's why hit makers do whatever's necessary to ensure that a song's production matches the quality of the song itself.

So if you want to make songs that sell, you're not done yet. The final ingredient of a hit song is the finishing touch, the one that leaves the mark of a craftsman. A&R people will recognize the attention to detail and know they're working with an experienced professional. Other songwriters will see the nuances of your work and respect your mastery of the craft. The average listener will suspect nothing at all but will be caught up in the relentless momentum of the song. To go all the way in maximizing a song's potential is to do the hidden things that distinguish a hit from a near-hit.

Finding the Dead Spots

A&R Guy: Don't you think the song gets a little boring right there? That one spot feels kind of dead.

Songwriter: That spot's not dead. It's just sleeping.

Most songwriters are sure that dead spot between the first chorus and the second verse or the lull in the middle of the bridge is really just a moment of rest, a little nap before the energy kicks in again. Isn't that what pacing and development are about? You have to give the audience a minute to breathe, right?

Not if the audience is my wife, surfing the channels on the car radio. In that instance, a moment's dead space will leave your song buried and forgotten before it has a chance to wake up. In a world that prefers relentless to restful, a songwriter must learn to identify any spot where the energy dips and fix it.

WARNING: Dead spots can kill you.

Dead spots are those moments when the natural flow of the song stalls, the rhythmic drive of the song is interrupted, or something repeats one too many times. The second a song hits a dead spot, the listeners' eyes glaze over and our minds wander, as we wait for the next section to start. For songwriters, the danger of the dead zone is that you often don't know you have one until it's too late, and your listener has dropped abruptly into the void. Eternal vigilance is your only protection.

Three Telltale Clues to Dead-Spot Spotting

The good news is that dead spots are not hard to identify, once you know what you're looking for. They may be as short as one or two measures, but they stand out when you're listening for them because...nothing happens. Here are a few surefire signs:

A MISSING MELODY Any time the primary melody stops, and no other melodic idea, like a secondary or hidden hook, emerges, you're likely to find a dead spot. Only rhythm can save you here. You'll need a very compelling groove to carry you through.

DISAPPEARING DRUMS Dropping the drums, or part of the drums, out of a track, even for one or two measures, creates an exciting and dramatic effect. It can provide a sudden change in texture, introduce a tone of intimacy, or set up a big moment to follow. But beware! A drum drop has its dangers. Should you keep the beat out a moment too long, with nothing else to draw the listener in, you can stall your engines in midflight. It's a quick trip down.

MORE OF THE SAME Dead spots don't always result from a lack of musical or lyrical events. Sometimes, they occur in spots where too much is happening. Too much repetition of a chorus or a riff, too many vocal ad-libs, or overly long instrumental solos carve out dead spots within cacophony—plenty is going on, but none of it is new. Patterns of repetition and change establish momentum. If something new occurs every eight measures, expectation and anticipation carry the audience through the song. If nothing new occurs, expectations will be disappointed and momentum will fade, regardless of how aggressive the track may be.

The Danger Zones

Given the common causes of dead spots, it's easy to deduce where such moments are likely to occur. Presumably, the chorus is the least likely spot, as pulling the drums or melody out of that particular section would be pretty unconventional. Likewise, a verse is unlikely to suffer from excessive repetition. Most often, dead spots turn up in the transitional sections: introductions, B-sections, interludes, or breakdowns. Here, a writer tends to focus on the song's forward direction, rather than on what's happening at the moment. By the time the song returns to the chorus, half the audience has jumped ship.

Slow, lengthy introductions are a particular pet peeve for A&R departments everywhere. In an effort to ease subtly into the groove, writers can kill a song before it even gets started. A twelve- or sixteen-bar introduction will never be heard—busy A&R people will press *fast forward* or, even more likely, *eject*. Introductions that lack a melodic motif waste an opportunity for a secondary hook. Worst of all, a weak introduction squanders those crucial first seconds, when a listener's mind is open and he or she has yet to deliver a verdict on the song.

The building of dynamics from section to section can present challenges as well. A B-section that takes two extra measures to pay off might build anticipation, or it might bring to mind the old Tin Pan Alley maxim: "Don't bore us, get to the chorus." An opening verse and chorus with no drums can be wonderfully sensitive and intimate, but it could also make the song virtually invisible when stuck between "Don't Cha" and "Lips of an Angel" on Top 40 radio. A breakdown, in which the instrumentation is dropped down to just drums or bass and percussion, is not the same in a pop song as it is in a dance remix. What is cool in a nightclub is dead space on the radio.

Of course, a song needs a natural ebb and flow to its dramatic development. But when you only have four minutes, there isn't much room for subtlety. Even a quiet, subdued section requires something to propel it forward.

The Big Mo

Once you've identified the dead spots in your song, you still need to fix them. Making things bigger or adding new elements to the arrangement won't always do the trick. Songs stall not because there is a lack of motion but rather from a loss of direction. Like a confused tourist trying to locate a familiar landmark in the middle of a busy city street, the song stops moving forward and hesitates for a few seconds. Unfortunately, that hesitation will cost you the one thing you can't afford to lose: The Big Mo.

The hook is how you catch 'em. Momentum is what keeps 'em on the line.

Momentum is an indispensable quality for any song, capable of covering up a multitude of other sins. Lyrics don't quite make sense? It doesn't matter, as long as the momentum keeps things moving ahead. Melody lacks that clever twist? Listeners won't complain, if they're caught up in the groove. Several forces within the song generate momentum: the physical energy of the rhythm, the forward motion of the chord progression, the dramatic development of the lyrical story, and the building of texture in the arrangement. Momentum is the motor that drives the song, as it holds the listener in a state of constant anticipation.

Do You Know Where You're Going To?

The secret to removing a dead spot is to restore the momentum. Just as a lost tourist has to recover his or her sense of direction, you have to define where your song is going and then find the path that will get you there. You can start by making a map.

The Songwriter's Challenge

It's important to begin the production process with a general vision of how the song's dramatic development will play out. Find a blank piece of graph paper, and let's chart the course:

1. Start by playing your song several times, as simply as possible—just a vocal with guitar, piano, or drum track. The natural emotional movement of the melody should be apparent, even in this basic form.

2. Any production or arrangement should follow the natural contour of the song. As you play or listen, notice where you feel the song's emotional peak, the dynamic crescendo, or the need for a more intimate delivery.

3. On your graph paper, make an *x/y* axis. On the *x*-axis, number each measure of the song, one box per measure. On the *y*-axis, number 1–10, starting from the bottom. This *y*-axis will represent the

emotional "intensity" level, with 1 being the least intense and 10 representing the emotional peak.

4. Find the peaks. Place a dot at the number 10, above the spot in the song that you feel is the true emotional climax. Usually this is the highest note of the melody (though not always) or the point of greatest urgency in the lyric.

5. Then go one step further, and in the same way mark the secondary peaks, which could range in intensity from 3 or 4 in the verse, to 7 or 8 in the bridge. Each section should have at least one secondary peak, even if it's very small. The chorus may have more than one.

6. In the same way, every song will have emotional dips, both large and small. At level 1 on the intensity meter, note the song's low point. This doesn't mean the worst part of the song; it means the moment of least intensity. Usually you'll find this point at the very beginning of the intro, right after the chorus, or after the bridge. Then mark the secondary dips as well.

7. Finally, connect the dots. If you've done it right, you should have what reads like an EKG of your song's natural pulse. From this, you should be able to visualize

clearly the rise and fall of the song's development. Play the song one more time and check your work.

Once you map the path of your song, you will have a better idea of how each section will function and, more important, where each section will lead. No matter how sparsely a particular section might be orchestrated, as long as it leads somewhere else, it will have momentum. As you construct your production, you'll need a kind of songwriter's navigation system, to recognize immediately when your song is veering off course.

If you have a dead spot in the introduction, it means that the section is not properly setting up what is to follow. Perhaps the chord progression in the introduction is not leading naturally to the progression in the verse. Maybe the secondary hook being used in the introduction doesn't prepare the listener for the verse melody. Maybe a spoken line in the introduction would set up the verse lyric and add a different perspective to the song's storyline.

Similarly, a dead spot in the bridge usually reveals a confusing dramatic arc. Is the bridge supposed to be the peak moment, before settling into a breakdown, or the climb up to a climax in the final chorus?

Coming out of the first chorus and back to the verse is always a dangerous part of the journey. If the drop-off is too gradual—the chorus tapering off into a low-intensity verse—the song's energy will dissipate. Conversely, if the chorus peaks dramatically in the final measure, then drops immediately into the verse, the shift will be too abrupt, obscuring the first few lines of the second verse lyric. You may need a short instrumental break, a bigger build to the chorus climax, or a "tag" section with a secondary hook to smooth the transition. As you search for solutions, refer to your original map. Every decision depends on where you are and where you're going.

Raising the Stakes

Once you've set the course, restored the momentum, and identified the major peaks in your song, you can go back and focus on building the tension, to give those high points as much impact as possible. Just as the author of a mystery story figures out the ending and writes backward from there, songwriters and producers identify a song's key emotional moments and then use a variety of traditional arranging devices to escalate the intensity and increase anticipation in the listener.

PLENTY OF UPS AND DOWNS Ascending or descending melodies, whether played by strings, horns, or built into the motion of the bass line, offer obvious strategies for moving audiences up and down the emotional staircase. Especially when the lines move in stepwise motion up or down the scale, a listener can't help being pulled along to the final destination. Use them when building from the B-section to the chorus or from the bridge to the final refrain.

A THICKENING PLOT A gradual thickening of the orchestration, with more instruments playing or singers singing, will always push up the intensity meter. Not only does it create a denser, more interesting musical bed, but it forces the singer to push harder to be heard. For example, a chorus is almost always bigger and more fully orchestrated than a verse. In the same way, if you're coming out of a climactic bridge into a wailing guitar solo, you want to do it with all guns blazing, and all instruments playing, to capture the emotional release you're after.

THE SOUND OF SILENCE Sometimes less is best. We've already touched on this trick. If you've tried it, you know how well it works. This could be a beat or more rest in the verse where everything comes to a sudden standstill (a favorite ploy of Swedish pop songwriters like Max Martin), a half-beat break that allows for a quick breath before the hook comes crashing in, or a tiny drop in instrumentation that sets up the big final line of the chorus.

The Songwriter's Challenge

Try each of the techniques I just described in the various transition points within your own song. Use one to bolster the B-section's build into the chorus. Try another to give the introduction a sense of motion and direction. Experiment to find which one will bring you out of the bridge most dramatically. Listen and absorb how these elements can restore life to what was a dead-spot desert.

Once you identify any two bars that do not constitute an emotional peak within the song, or do not build momentum leading to an emotional peak, you can pronounce them officially "dead." You better either cut those sections out entirely or figure out some way to get them moving. It's a little like pole-vaulting: If a song is going to rise to the level of a hit, it can't afford anything that slows it down. To make that ultimate leap, a song needs all the momentum it can get.

Setting the Bar

At the start of this book, the question was presented: "What secrets do consistent hit songwriters know that the legions of other aspiring writers do not?" We've explored several answers to that question, including the various "hit" formulas, the function of hit songs within the music industry, and the ingredients that make up a hit song. Still, there is one answer that underlies all the others. Conveniently, we've held that best-kept secret until the end. The most important thing that hit songwriters know, but most developing songwriters do not, is this:

Hit songwriters know how high the quality bar is set. Moreover, they will do whatever is necessary to reach it.

Writing songs can be fun. Occasionally, writing a hit song can be an easy, almost magical process. However, for professional songwriters, it's also a job. It's a job upon which millions of dollars of record company investment and an artist's career may rest. Understandably, serious songwriters treat the endeavor with respect.

Writing hit songs consistently is not easy. It is an extremely competitive job in one of the world's most competitive businesses. As I said at the outset, to create something that is different, but not too different, fresh and long lasting, with both good form and real substance, is the ultimate challenge. Virtually every proven hit maker across all genres boasts the same characteristic: a stubborn, obsessive, sometimes exasperating refusal to settle for anything that falls short of the mark.

"My whole thing is, I want to win," acknowledges Irv Gotti, the mastermind behind The Inc. and artists like Ashanti and Ja Rule. "If someone calls me [to do a track], I'm giving them a hundred and ten percent, because I want to make hits—and that's it! That's the only thing that matters. Either you make hits in this game, or you get the hell out of this game, and I don't want to get out yet."[*]

---

[*] From "Behind the Boards," Rap/Hip-Hop section, *Billboard* (November 2002). Excerpt used with permission of Nielsen Business Media, Inc.

If that sounds cocky, don't be surprised. Most successful song-writers are confident of their ability and secure in the quality of their work. When they come to my office to play their song, they don't usually ask me if it's a hit—they tell me. They feel comfort-able promoting their work, not because they are arrogant or naive but rather because they know that they have already put their song through a quality-control testing process far more rigorous than anything a record company or radio station could administer. These top writers have already faced the harshest critic the indus-try can muster: themselves.

If you need someone else to find the dead spots in your song, you're not yet ready to be a hit songwriter.

> The ability to listen to your own work objectively is perhaps the most essential songwriting skill of all.

Without this skill, you will never allow yourself to be chal-lenged to reach beyond your initial ideas. If you can't recognize the clichés in your own lyrics, you'll never push yourself to cre-ate something original. If you don't hear that your melody is stagnant, you won't force yourself to come up with a twist. When you're not aware that a song feels out-of-date, you won't find a way to make it contemporary. Great songwriters have an eagle's eye for spotting problems, an unforgiving set of standards, and an unstoppable determination to fix anything that falls short.

Taking Criticism...Critically

Given all that, most hit songwriters don't have much need for criticism from outside. Nevertheless, they remain open to the comments of others. They listen to what others think, without being destroyed or angered by it or unreasonably resistant to it. However, they don't accept blindly whatever criticism is made and immediately begin rewriting.

Criticism is always a "take it or leave it" proposition. The challenge lies in knowing which comments to accept and which ones to dismiss. If you bring exacting standards to your own work, an isolated comment from a casual listener should not carry much weight. On the other hand, if that comment confirms your own misgivings, or is echoed by others whom you respect, then it's worth considering. If the same criticism comes repeatedly from industry professionals, then it has to be acknowledged. You don't have to change your work to accommodate the criticism—it is, after all, your song. Nevertheless, you do have to accept that the collective verdict has been rendered: Unless you fix the issues in question, there will be real challenges to the commercial success of the song.

Manager and former A&R executive Gerry Griffith once told me a story about a meeting between Clive Calder, the founder of Jive Records, and Clive Davis, the legendary record label chief of Arista Records. Clive Calder had just played what was to be one of his first releases on the Jive label, a song called "European

Queen." He was leaving the office when Clive Davis called after him. "Why don't you do different versions of it in different territories? Maybe 'African Queen' for Africa, and 'European Queen' for Europe," he suggested. Clive Calder, a man with pretty strong ideas of his own, thought about it for a moment. He liked the concept.

Months later, the song came out with a different title for each territory. It was a novel approach, but it didn't really work. At least, not until the company decided to try one other version of the song, "Caribbean Queen (No More Love on the Run)." Sung by new artist Billy Ocean, it became a worldwide hit and the song that launched the Jive Records label. The moral is this: Even the most knowledgeable opinions are sometimes right, and sometimes wrong, and sometimes a little bit of both. The best way to take them is with an open mind and a willingness to adapt.

It's Not Over Until You Rewrite

Admittedly, adapting is the hard part. It's easy to accept criticism. It's hard to rewrite. Yet there is no use finding weak spots or listening to suggestions if you won't try to make the necessary changes. Every professional understands the necessity of going back to the drawing board, to make something better, more commercial, or more appropriate for a specific project.

Not every rewrite is intended to address a flaw in the original. Music exists as a product in the cold, hard commercial world, which often requires changes to be made for practical reasons, rather than wholly artistic ones. If a song could work for a Radio

Disney artist, except for the presence of a suggestive lyric line, then that line must change. When the TV star turned recording artist can't hit the high note in the bridge, then the melody has to change. By resisting the realities of the marketplace, songwriters demonstrate their inexperience, rather than their integrity.

Perhaps you don't believe the change that's been requested will improve the song. You may be right. Try it anyway. Most of the time, you can find a solution that satisfies everyone. If after a reasonable effort you still feel that nothing measures up to the original, then you can rest knowing you've exhausted all other alternatives. A song is not a piece of china that can be broken and never pieced back together. If a new idea for the song doesn't work, you simply won't use it. No harm, no foul.

When I was at Zomba Music, the Backstreet Boys song "I Want It That Way" underwent numerous rewrites by the writers Max Martin and Andreas Carlsson in an attempt to fix the opening lines, which rhymed "fire" and "desire"—a cliché guaranteed to set A&R teeth grinding. Finally, a new version of the verse was recorded, mixed, and edited to replace the offending lines. Only when the album neared the mastering stage was it decided that the original version, despite the old cliché, was still the stronger opening verse. Probably, it was an accurate call, as the song went on to be one of the biggest hits of the decade and fuel the sales of over 20 million albums around the world.

The point of this story is not that clichés are good, or that criticism often results in fixing what wasn't broken in the first place. The message is that if Max Martin and Andreas Carlsson will try to make changes, so can you. In a business where popular tastes continually change and everyone has an opinion, the ability to adapt is the ultimate survival skill.

THE INSIDE TRACK

Those Magic Moments
Daniel Glass

GLASSNOTE RECORDS

From his start as the DJ at New York's legendary nightclub Regine's, to his role as label president at EMI Records North America, Universal Records, and Artemis Records, to his current position as founder and CEO of Glassnote Records, music industry veteran Daniel Glass has been involved with hit records ranging from Wilson Phillips to Billy Idol, from Jesus Jones to Secondhand Serenade. The determination to discover the small detail that makes something great, to rewrite and revise until a song reaches its maximum potential is a quality that Glass witnessed in his earliest days in the industry.

DANIEL GLASS: I remember being at discos like Le Jardin when I was young and seeing Barry White in the DJ booth. I didn't really know who he was. Later I went to Minneapolis and I saw Prince in the DJ booth. I asked the DJs after they left, "What were they doing there?" They just wanted to see how people reacted to the songs. They would go home and change their records—put on more bass, more top end, remix, extend the break. They absolutely needed to know how the dance floor felt.

I was just recently having this discussion with people, saying, "Why do hits all sound the same?" Not that they're all in the same musical style. But we were listening to a song and we just said, "Man, that one's got the whole thing." It's that immediate quality that just jumps out at you. It's the writing and the mastering and the mixing—it's that je ne sais quoi. The masters—the Ahmet Erteguns, the Bob Krasnows, the Berry Gordys—they knew it. They'd be in the studio, three o'clock in the morning, and they'd know, "We got the magic." It starts with the song, but then all of a sudden the magic happens. It could be the smallest detail, it could be the tambourine or the shaker, but there would just be something about that record.

All of the hits, in any genre, you pile 'em up together and they sound magical. Not once they're successful, but when they start. Kelly Clarkson's "Since U Been Gone" had that. So did the R.E.M. song, "Losing My Religion." On that one it was the lyric that got me. You hear those songs as a professional and you say, "My competitor's record sounds great. I gotta try harder."

Having seen firsthand the challenges facing the traditional record business, Glass has positioned his new label to take advantage of all of today's opportunities for digital distribution and online promotion. Even as he notes the challenges confronting the music industry, he remains a steadfast believer in the power of a hit song.

DANIEL GLASS: It used to be that a hit was a song that got a lot of requests on the radio station and sold a lot of records. Today, that's still very, very important, but there are new forms of exposure and media that bring you into the hit area. You could have a hit song from a video game. You could have a YouTube phenomenon because of the song combined with the video. The word of mouth that spreads a hit is happening in a different form. What has not changed is what makes up the magic of a hit song—those intangibles, the emotional connection of the beat, the melody, the hook, and the lyric with the listener.

I remember working the first Wilson Phillips single to radio and being in the booth with a radio DJ who'd been playing the record. He asked me to listen to the phone calls coming into the station. So I heard a late-night call in Memphis, from a girl who was having real problems in her life. She was crying, and she said, "That song is getting me through—when I hear 'Hold on for one more day.'" That's the connection that a hit song makes. That's why they continue to matter to us.

The Myth, the Miracle, and the Making of a Hit

Nothing rankles a professional songwriter more than the myth of the idyllic songwriting existence—that gauzy picture of a stress-free atmosphere in which creative souls spend their days lost in the bliss of effortless inspiration. Veteran writers know too well the relentless drive required to create hit records in the pressure-cooker environment of the music industry. None would dispute the necessity of inspiration, but neither would they discount the effort that goes into polishing that diamond in the rough.

"An idea may pop into your head, but that's just a place to start. That's just the first flash of the miracle," warns Sharon Vaughn. The rest is the work of giving form to that "beautiful disaster," as Darrell Brown called it. It's that dedication to detail that separates the master craftsman from those with stars in their eyes.

"I find that the biggest challenge with young writers is a sense of entitlement," Brown continues. "You work with so many new writers and you're seduced by their talent, until you get in the room with them and you go, 'Oh my gosh, they think because they're talented that's all they need to be.' It's just not enough. The professionalism has to be there."

If you hadn't seen it before, now you know: The road to a hit record is a long, precarious journey that demands as much effort as inspiration. Along the way, you'll come across A&R people chasing that elusive "first single," radio programmers running research, and music marketing teams fighting their way through the clutter. You'll face the conflicting demands for something "different, but not too different," trendy but timeless, "formula" but not formulaic.

Finally, it will come down to you, in your living room or recording studio, and what you can do with your guitar, piano, drum machine, or voice. Every writer has the same basic tools at his or her disposal: lyrics, melody, rhythm, and hooks. Success depends largely on how far and deep you will go in searching for new lyric concepts, innovative rhythms, a melodic twist, or a secondary hook. Certainly, your results will be determined in part by the quality of what you have to express. But much will also rest on the way that you express it—the care that you bring to structuring your song, refining it, and restructuring it as many times, and in as many ways, as it takes to get it right.

I've always laughed at how songwriting is depicted in the movies or on television. The scene inevitably begins with a shot of crumpled paper being tossed in a garbage can. A man sits at the piano, rubbing his head in frustration. Searching for an idea, he strings two, then three notes together at the keyboard. Someone else hums a little melody quietly in another room. The man looks up from his piano...then, instantly, we cut to the picture of a superstar, delivering the now-familiar hit song to a cheering crowd.

Don't be fooled. Few hit songs arrive fully developed at birth, and many might be unrecognizable in their earliest form. A song is a hit because a songwriter made it that way, one creative decision at a time. If, in the end, your song sounds effortless when it plays on the radio, it's merely a testament to the skill and determination of the person who wrote it, and rewrote it, into perfection.

Conclusion
The Big Final Chorus

One day while I was finishing up the final chapters of this book, I found myself sharing a New York City subway ride with a somewhat overexcited junior high school choir. The group was on their way to give a performance and had the pent-up energy and pre-show jitters of divas waiting to take the stage of the Metropolitan Opera.

Like storm clouds gathering out of nowhere and finally bursting, the choir kids suddenly broke into song—forty young students giving an impromptu performance of Natasha Bedingfield's hit "Unwritten," in the hot and crowded confines of a subway car, singing *"Feel the rain on your skin..."*

Even a group of jaded New York straphangers could hardly stifle their smiles. Yet the real surprise was what followed. Having finished their first song, the youthful choir then segued into the song that I've cited so many times in this book, Smokey Robinson and Ronald White's classic, "My Girl." Over forty years after the song was written, it still sounded fresh and vibrant, as relevant to these young people as it was to their parents and grandparents. I even caught a few other passengers singing along.

Daniel Glass was right. All hits sound the same. Whether it's "Unwritten" or "My Girl," "Stand by Me," or "Beautiful Girls," they all speak the same language. Whether they come from a transistor radio, a boom box, an iPod, or an eighth-grade choir in a subway car, they all work the same magic. In a world that's increasingly fragmented and temporary, hit songs communicate in a way that's universal and timeless.

The industry needs hits because they cut through the marketing clutter and sell records. Artists need hits because they define identity and launch careers. As a society, we need hits because our lives need a soundtrack. Just as the ancients had their epic poems, and the pioneers had their songs to sing around the campfire, we have our hits, those songs that capture our experience, tell us who we are, and bind us together in a community.

There are those in the media who would have you believe that in this age of specialized markets, file sharing, and unlimited access to music of every type and quality, the industry is no longer reliant on a big, breakthrough single for commercial success. So far, it seems to be just the opposite. There is no clutter like that of the new media, and not surprisingly, it takes a hit song to break through it. Careers launched from MySpace and YouTube, from Colbie Caillat to Soulja Boy, have been driven by conventional "singles"—songs that were different but not too different, with a typical pop song form and a bit of substance that set them apart. In fact, as the music industry witnesses the decline of the album format and begins to revive formats like the single song release and the three- or four-song EP, only the strongest songs will survive.

"In the future, if there are going to be albums, or some kind of collection of songs, whether it's three or six or whatever—every song is going to have to be good. We'll probably see songs doled out one or two at a time, like the fifties and sixties, with the singles being bundled together with concert tickets and a T-shirt. If that's the case, then on a songwriting level, the album filler is a thing of the past," Daniel Glass predicts.

There is nothing in this book that can substitute for natural musical talent, an intuitive melodic sensibility, or a unique way of looking at the world. What I've tried to provide is some guidance in focusing that talent and shaping that creativity into a format that will be viable for the industry and accessible to the general public.

Even for immensely gifted artists and songwriters, the music business can often seem like a frustrating maze of dead ends and closed doors. But once you understand what the decision makers behind those closed doors are looking for, and you learn to structure and produce your music to satisfy those demands, you will find that the doors once locked tightly are suddenly swinging open.

In over twenty years in the music business, I've seen it happen again and again. An unknown songwriter shows up out of nowhere, with nothing but one song that feels like a hit. It's never easy and often takes longer than it should, but inevitably, phones begin to ring. A manager calls a publisher, "You need to hear this…" The publisher calls the record companies. An A&R person calls a producer. Pretty soon, everyone in the industry is buzzing about the hot new kid in town with a killer first single. The more the industry changes, the more some things remain the same.

A band with one surefire single will be signed to a record contract long before a more experienced band with ten pretty good songs. A songwriter with one hit on the charts will be offered a publishing deal before another songwriter with a dozen album cuts. Hits are the currency of the music business, and as such, they rarely remain undiscovered. If you've got a genuine hit, someone will take notice.

Probably, it won't happen often. Even for successful songwriters, the big classic hit song is a career highlight, not an everyday occurrence. But if you set your sights on creating songs that make an impact, establish an identity, and communicate a concept, your standards will rise, and your performance will rise to meet them.

"We want to make a masterpiece every time, but that's just not possible," acknowledges Mikkel Eriksen of Stargate. "You have to make ten songs to come up with one really, really great one."

I hope this book can provide some insight into what distinguishes a great song from a merely good one. I've tried to offer some ideas for how to raise the level of your songs from good to great. But most of all, I hope I've encouraged you to make the effort, to strive to create songs that not only express but also communicate your unique perspective to a larger audience. We need those songs—whether we're industry executives looking for the first single from a new artist or a group of eager young singers on a New York subway car. As my publisher used to tell me on the way to the studio, "Write a hit." We'll all be glad you did.

Index

Index

Index

Index

Index

Index

Index

Index

Index

About the Author

ERIC BEALL is the author of *Making Music Make Money: An Insider's Guide to Becoming Your Own Music Publisher* as well as a respected music industry insider. He has worked with a variety of artists, songwriters, and producers, ranging from the Backstreet Boys and Britney Spears to Sarah McLachlan, Billy Mann, and Stargate.

Prior to joining the executive ranks, Eric wrote and produced the pop hits "Nothin' My Love Can't Fix" for Joey Lawrence and "Carry On" by Martha Wash, as well as songs for Diana Ross, The Jacksons, Safire, Samantha Fox, Brenda K. Starr and many others. He is a frequent lecturer and teacher at music industry conventions and seminars and a teacher and course designer for Berkleemusic at the prestigious Berklee College of Music. He blogs at ericbeall.berkleemusicblogs.com.